Ten Vital Questions

What To Ask When Trying To Find Your Ideal Business

GORDON VAN WECHEL

ISBN-10: 1500352489
ISBN-13: 978-1500352486

DEDICATION

This book is dedicated to my parents, Gordon and Lynn, who didn't teach me much about business, but helped me learn everything I needed to know about a living a life of service and happiness.

CONTENTS

Gordon Van Wechel

Forward to the Second Edition.

When I first wrote Ten Vital Questions three years ago, my primary objective was to provide hopeful entrepreneurs with some thought provoking ideas that may not have occurred to them. Our nation was about four years into a serious recession, with no relief in sight. As a marketing consultant I found myself talking with an increasing number of "corporate veterans" who had been downsized or their employers had gone out of business.

These conversations convinced me that a career spent working for a large corporation, no matter a person's rank or title when their career was over, was remarkably poor preparation for the life of an entrepreneur. No matter how challenging a situation these men and women had faced in their previous business life, there was always the safety net of other staff people and the stability of the company.

For most new business owners those don't exist. You can't delegate tasks you don't want to do because there is no one to delegate them to; as the owner you wear all the hats. There isn't a "company" backing you up...you are the company. It doesn't matter what department you ran before, now you are all of the departments: HR, Purchasing, Sales, Accounting, Marketing, and most days the janitor too.

I wrote the book to give these well meaning and hard working people some insights into the world they were about to enter. If conversations with readers of that first edition are any indication, my effort was largely successful. Several related that they had changed the category of business they were considering after reading the book. Others told of saving thousands of dollars by not making some mistakes they were headed for before reading it. More than a few decided not to start their own business after all.

In offering this revised and updated edition of Ten Vital Questions, my purpose is largely the same. The stagnant economy remains, and good people are still looking for alternatives to provide security for their families. The need for this information still exists.

In this edition I have updated many of the references to the current time, including the experiences of several recent clients. Perhaps the biggest change is that I'm suggesting three business models that meet the criteria suggested by the Ten Vital Questions. These are Network Marketing, Internet Based Affiliate Marketing, and Consulting.

Whether you are considering starting a business of your own, or already have one, asking yourself the Ten Vital Questions can be a game changing exercise for you. So often as business owners we are too close to our business to know what is really happening around us. The Ten Vital Questions demand that you step back and see with new eyes.

I hope that you find the Ten Vital Questions to be valuable.

To Your Success!

Gordon

Part One:

The Ten Vital Questions

Gordon Van Wechel

The Ten Vital Questions

1. What can you afford to invest?

2. What ongoing overhead is needed?

3. Does the business require you to hire employees or inventory product to resell?

4. Do you have to do any invoicing, collections or carry any accounts receivable?

5. Does the business have proven systems for you to follow?

6. What is the demand for your product or service?

7. How much competition is there?

8. Are there niches to market to?

9. What is the company history? Who are you getting into bed with?

10. Is there an opportunity to get wealthy with residual income?

Gordon Van Wechel

Chapter 1

"And the company made a massive profit in the fourth quarter and they all lived happy ever after."

Preparing To Go Into Business

At the time I'm writing this, over 50% of the new businesses that are started in the United States fail within the first two years. More than 80% don't survive until their 5th birthday. Why do you suppose that is?

Well meaning budding entrepreneurs will make an "all in" bet on their venture. They'll mortgage their home, cash in retirement accounts, and borrow from relatives to get the doors open. That's when the real work begins. For the most part, the new business owner is a hard worker, wearing multiple hats as he or she attempts to become successful.

But the overwhelming majority of these hopeful business people fail. Why?

In my conversations with hundreds of business owners over the years I see two primary causes for failure. First, not being crystal clear on what they want to accomplish; and second, not having a realistic plan for achieving their goals.

The fact that you are reading this book means that you are very serious about finding a business that is a good fit for you. The obvious question is why? Why do you want a business for yourself? What do you hope to accomplish financially by having your own business? What is your expectation about the lifestyle of a small business owner? If you have a family, are they going to be involved in the enterprise with you?

I told you that this was going to be a "working book." That is, I'm going to ask you to do some thinking and tasks other than just reading my words. That starts now. So grab a legal pad and pen, and then pick up the book again.

I'm serious! Go get a paper and pen so you can make some notes. And keep them handy.

Let's begin by asking yourself the question: "Why do I want to be in a business of my own?" Take some time and think about it. To stimulate your thinking, here are some common answers:

> I have a great idea and want to build a business around it
> Business owners make a lot more money than employees
> My father/mother owned a business and I want them to be proud of me
> I hate my job
> I've always dreamed of having a company of my own
> I want to leave a legacy for my kids
> I'm not employable (age, legal issues, a perceived disability...)

Do any of these apply to you?

Here's another question important for any business owner: Do you have written goals? I understand that we all have goals, and most of us can articulate them quite clearly. But are they written down anywhere? If they're not, then they are not goals, just hopes.

For those of you who have taken the time to think through and write down your goals, I have another question. Have you written goals only for your business? What about the other areas of your life? Have you considered goals for your family, health, spiritual and intellectual development? The reality is that you won't have your "business life" and "the rest of your life." So investing a lot of time developing business goals without considering how your business integrates with the other important categories of life is short sighted.

Here's a formula that I have used for years, and have watched friends and clients successfully implement as well.

First, I ask what are my goals for the next 12 months in each of these areas of my life?

1. Financial/business

2. Spiritual

3. Health/Physical

4. Family

5. Personal Development

These are not in a particular order, nor are they the only categories you might select from or choose to include in your personal list...they're just a guideline. I like to work in 12 month blocks of time, then create goals for the next three months based on those 12 month time chunks.

For example, let's say you have a goal to run a marathon sometime in the next year. In March you learn that a marathon has been scheduled for the end of September in a town within a reasonable drive from your home. Of course you'll begin training right away, 26 miles is a long way to run! But you will allocate significantly more time to race preparation in the three months leading up to the event itself. So for those three months you may not focus as much on Personal Development goals just due to the extra time allocated to training runs.

When the race is complete, you would likely spend less time the following three months on Health/Physical goals and "catch up" in some of the other areas.

This process is not "calendar dependent." That is, you don't have to wait until January to begin. Start now, begin to set goals in the areas that are meaningful to you for the next twelve months. Then work on the next quarter and develop an action plan based on your goals.

What does this have to do with starting a business?

Everything! It is the critical first step in even deciding if you want to be in a business for yourself. Owning a business is not an easy task. The time it takes to be successful in the early years can be considerable. There is often a great deal of personal stress associated with starting and managing an enterprise. Is that what you really want?

Or are your personal goals such that you can find satisfaction by some means other than starting a business?

Alex (not his real name) came to me last year. We had met socially and he knew I worked with new business owners. He wanted to start a business, and was looking at several franchise opportunities. As we talked about his "why" for going into his own company, it was clear to me that the motivation was based more on frustration with his current corporate job than any strong desire to create a new company.

When we talked about how he spent his time away from the office, his priorities were very clear. He was in his second marriage and was committed to investing the time that this relationship needed. Additionally, he and his wife had an eight year old son, and Alex coached the soccer team and helped his son with reading skills every evening after dinner.

Over a few conversations Alex determined that what he

needed was a new challenge at work, not a new business. He eventually accepted an offer from another company to manage a department and is not only happier, he has excelled for this employer and found a great deal of personal satisfaction that was lacking in his previous job.

When thinking about getting into a business for self keep in mind all the components of your life and lifestyle. The first two years of starting a new business take a great deal of time and can be quite stressful. Malcolm Forbes said, "start your business with the end in mind. Will this business give me the lifestyle I want?"

Being crystal clear on all of your goals, not just business goals, is the first best way to avoid business failure.

Here are some other thoughts as you develop your business goals:

1. At its essence, business is about creating value in the world and being compensated because you have made people's lives better. Business is about getting what you want by giving people what they want or need. Does your business idea make people's lives better by giving them what they want or need?

2. Be a specialist by offering something others don't or won't. Make sure that your specialty is easily

understood. We often call this a Unique Selling Proposition (USP) and without it you can't separate yourself from your competition. Does your business idea have a clear advantage over the competition when it comes to giving the customers what they want or need?

3. There is a saying something like, "do what you love and the money will follow." That is mostly crap! The business graveyard is full of well meaning hobbyists who tried to take their passion and make a business out of it. Or someone who took Grandma's recipes and opened a café. While it is important to enjoy what you are choosing do spend most of your day doing, you also need to make sure it really is a viable business vehicle.

4. Avoid commodity businesses. A commodity is a business where there is little or no difference between suppliers, so you have to compete on price. It's difficult to make a good living when you constantly have to shave your margin to get the sale.

4a. Don't try to fight big business! You will never be able to compete with the big box stores when it comes to buying capability or staying power. If your business idea can be duplicated at Wal-Mart or Amazon or Ebay look for something else.

5. Think carefully about market timing. Look for trends,

consider demographics. I'm part of what is known as the "baby boom" generation—one of 78 million people. When we were born the baby food industry boomed, as we grew up schools were built. My generation drove the real estate boom, and more recently contributed to that industries bust. Now that many of us are turning 60, the wellness industry is heating up.

Is the product or service that you're thinking about building a business around in front of a market wave? Or has it already been swamped?

6. Can you create business systems for your company? Think for a minute about what characterizes a franchise? Systems. That is why people buy a franchise, they are a proven business model where procedures have already been worked out. Even that doesn't guarantee success, lots of franchises go out of business every week. But the more you can create systems for your business the better your odds, and the more you will be able to train and trust key employees to manage when you are not on site.

The second reason such a high percentage of new businesses fail is because they do not have a realistic plan to accomplish the goals that were set. That's right, they don't have a comprehensive business plan, a roadmap, to follow in the early months.

There are some really good books in the marketplace that will help you write a business plan, as well as software programs developed for this task. Lots of business consultants will be happy to help you, for a fee. You can go to the SBA and get guidance, or contact SCORE through the SBA and learn from seasoned business professionals.

I'm not going to try to condense this important topic to just a couple of pages when there are excellent resources out there for you to use. I do want to stress one aspect of the process that is often glossed over by many business plan authors. That is the idea of determining the existence of your market before investing a lot of time or money developing a plan.

What do I mean by that? Are there enough people in your area who buy what you want to offer to justify having a business? If there isn't a decent size market you shouldn't go into the business! That is often what my clients don't want to hear, but it's too important to ignore. Let me give you a personal example.

When I moved to New Mexico several years ago I quickly realized that I was at "ground zero" for the turquoise jewelry industry. Most of the active turquoise mines in the world are within a couple of hundred miles of my home. Native American artisans and silversmiths are also close by, as well as wholesalers who consolidate production from the reservations. I could purchase across several price ranges and quality brackets under very favorable terms.

I decided that I would evaluate setting up a store on Ebay and go into the Western jewelry business. As I analyzed the competition I quickly realized that many were selling an inferior product that was mined and produced in China. However, there were several stores selling large inventories of American Southwest jewelry. They had all of the products I was considering selling: rings, bracelets, watch bands, chokers, earrings, and necklaces. Here was the best part: because I was so close to the source of supply, I could offer jewelry in my Ebay store for 60% of what others were selling at and still make a substantial profit. Sounds like a no brainer, right?

Wrong.

Ebay offers an analysis of what has actually sold through the system, and at what price, for the previous 90 days. This is critically important data. When I analyzed the "sold statistics" I realized that while there were some sales being made, there were clearly not enough to support the time it would take to manage this business. Yes, I could hire someone to keep up the virtual storefront and process orders, but that would further reduce profit. Meanwhile, it would be my money tied up in inventory and my time spent visiting the wholesale outlets to buy. These competing stores on Ebay were quite impressive, with several hundred auctions and "buy it now" sales in progress. What I learned after investigating was that very few of these listings ever sold.

Here's the point. If there is not a strong marketplace of buyers who have money to spend, and a proven track record of spending for similar products, you probably don't have a business worth developing.

A couple of final thoughts before we jump into the Ten Vital Questions.

There are three reasons typically given for why someone doesn't go into business, even when they have a good idea. These are fear of failure, lack of capital, and lack of knowledge. All of these are valid, but can be overcome by a motivated person.

If one of these reasons is holding you back, you're in the right place. I've written this book to give a strong sense of confidence to someone fearful about going into business. With knowledge comes confidence, and my goal is to give you a clear understanding of the pitfalls, and how to step right over them and be successful.

I'm a firm believer in sweat equity instead of bank or

borrowed money equity. I started one of my companies with $5000 that I borrowed from my dad. Four years later we did over $3 million in sales. It can be done with the right plan, and yes, I paid my father back.

Sometimes people fail to follow through on their ideas because they don't have a way to determine whether their concept has a chance of being successful. In the following pages I'm going to give you a guide for planning and starting a business. With the properly planned structure in place, you can move forward with confidence to market analysis, business planning, capitalization, and a successful launch of your enterprise.

If you've ever participated in a personality evaluation workshop you have probably seen the four quadrant method. This is where an x and y axis are drawn on the board, and each of the resulting squares is assigned a name that describes a personality type. One system divides people into Driver, Analytical, Expressive, and Amiable social styles. Another uses animals to convey the same concept: eagle, owl, peacock and dove.

As I've worked with entrepreneurs in their current business, and "soon to be" entrepreneurs in planning their future business, I've developed my own variation on this segmentation. Mine is based on "action style" rather than social style. Here they are:

1. Ready, Aim, Ready, Aim, Ready, Aim. This person is extremely thorough, investigating all the possibilities and developing contingency plans for each. In fact, they're so thorough that they never get past the planning stage and launch their business.

2. Fire, Fire, Fire. This person is the consummate entrepreneur, full of really good ideas. They have so many that they start one project, the get a new idea and move over to start it. Then, just as they're ready to go back to the first one, yup, here comes another. Lots of things get started, very few every completed.

3. Ready, Fire, Aim. For much of my career, this would describe me. Get the idea, do some preliminary research, pull the trigger, then deal with issues as they come up. In fact, most "serial entrepreneurs" are like this. The excitement of launch easily overcomes the frustration that results from partial planning.

A couple of years ago, serial entrepreneur Michael Masterson published a book entitled, Ready-Fire-Aim where he recommended this management style. It works for the experienced entrepreneur, but can be deadly for the neophyte.

4. Ready, Aim, Fire. If this is your first foray into the world of business for self, this is the path you want to follow. The Ready steps include evaluating yourself to

make sure you understand and are prepared for what is coming. You've looked at all the options and carefully considered the type of business opportunity that will fit your lifestyle desires and risk tolerance.

Once you have taken into account the relevant personal factors and are ready to focus on the business type you want, it is time to Aim.

This Aim stage is where you carefully analyze the variety of opportunities that interest you. Use the ten questions in this book to stimulate your thinking and challenge your assumptions about each. The goal at this stage is to develop a laser like focus.

Then it's time to fire. Like a competitive marksman in the Olympics, you take a deep breath, exhale completely, then squeeze the trigger. You launch your business!

This more methodical approach is exactly the right one for the person considering starting their first business, or who has a failure or two under their belt and wants to do it right this time. It is for you that this book is written.

Gordon Van Wechel

Chapter 2

"....so don't commit to anything until you know who to blame if things go wrong."

Question #1: What can you afford to invest?

The first consideration any of us have to make when thinking about starting a new business is a realistic appraisal of how much money we can raise to initially fund the enterprise. It's important to decide this right from the beginning so you are not tempted to try and leverage into a business you really can't afford.

Making this decision early and "setting it in concrete" will also help you stand firm when a business broker or seller of an opportunity tries to convince you what a "really great deal" they're offering you—even if it is "just $100,000 more than you budgeted."

You also have to keep in mind that there are actually two financial investments to take into account: first is the cost to buy and start the business. Equally important is the second, the continuing overhead you'll have to spend during the time it takes to get your business to profitability. Most of us will underestimate both of these. I'm going to talk more about the second of these, operating expenses, in the next chapter.

Let's look at an example. A franchise, say a pizza delivery company, will typically require a minimum investment just for the right to use the name and systems provided by the franchisor. That's just the beginning. Then there is identifying a location to conduct your business, attending company training, getting plans and specs approved by both the franchisor and the city you are doing business in, acquiring building permits (which never happen as quickly as you need them to!), completing the build out necessary to customize the site your new company specifications (ditto!), purchasing equipment and getting it installed, buying inventory, and a myriad of other expenses that are part of starting a new business.

That is just to get to the place where you are able to open the doors to the public. Then you'll have rent, advertising, utilities, payroll, taxes, and numerous other day to day costs of being in business. You'll need at least six months of these expenses as cash in your account before you open. You can't assume that the public will beat a path to your door in these first months. Even if you have an extensive marketing budget it takes time to penetrate all but the most unique markets. Be prepared for some very lean months in the early days.

Even a franchise that you can operate out of your home or add on to your existing business will have significant start up costs and cash reserve requirements. So while you might be able to minimize or eliminate all together some of the costs I've identified, there are still many expenses to consider.

Another reason for realistically assessing your financial capability is to narrow your search for a business quickly. If you can only invest, say, $80,000; you can eliminate from your consideration literally thousands of businesses right from the beginning...any business where the estimated start up costs are more than $80,000 are off the table. Actually, something less than $80,000 because you'll need to have operating reserves for the first six months from that initial investment pool as well.

Making a realistic evaluation of what you can afford to invest is the all important first step towards owning a business that becomes successful and profitable.

What happens when you sit down and evaluate all of your assets and potential sources of funding and it becomes clear that you have no chance to afford the type of business you wanted? Time to cash it in and go look for a job?

Not necessarily.

Getting money for starting a business is difficult, but need not be impossible. In fact, the process of finding money for starting a business can serve as a refining fire for your business idea. It will force you to think through each aspect of the business clearly and objectively. Just because you "think something will work" isn't going to be enough for a funding source. They are going to want to see hard facts based on the realities of the marketplace. If you can successfully navigate this gauntlet and get the commitment of a financial investor, then you have made a huge step toward creating a successful enterprise.

So how do you do this?

It all begins with your business plan. This is your road

map. The discipline of creating such a plan will help you know exactly how much money you will need at each stage of the process, when it will be needed, and how an investor is going to get his/her money back. Go to the library or book store and find a workbook that will help you with this task. For a valuable free resource go to www.sba.gov. This is the Small Business Administration website. There is a link "starting a business" that will have additional links to a description of the process and even some forms and templates you can use to create your own plan.

If you are not a person given to detail then get some help with this process. I guarantee you that anyone who is going to carefully consider investing with you is going to want a great deal of proof showing that you've thoroughly investigated your idea and are worthy of their cash. This is one of those times where you only get one opportunity to make a good first impression. Don't risk the opportunity by showing up with an incomplete plan.

Make sure your business plan includes a start-up cost detail, cash flow projection, and a break even analysis. It is helpful to complete the break even analysis with at least three different sales scenarios: what you expect the sales to be each month in the first few months, then another spreadsheet with sales that are at least 25% less than you expect, and a third that are an equal amount more than you project. A typical investor will pay the most attention to the "less than what I think" numbers, and probably even subtract from them before arriving at their own interpretation of your business plan.

Don't be insulted by this process. That is one of the reasons they have the money to invest!

The Language of Business Finance

If you have not worked with commercial lending before there are some terms that are used in the industry. Whether you're dealing with a bank, insurance company, investment group, or private capital individual you will want to be familiar with these.

A **credit score** is the numerical expression based on a statistical analysis of your credit files. It is used as an indication of your credit worthiness, and is typically obtained from the one or more of the three national credit reporting bureaus.

A lender will use this score to evaluate the potential risk of doing business with you. To some extent your credit score influences your interest rate and the maximum amount of the loan you can obtain. A private lender may not require you to provide a credit report or score, and will place less emphasis on this tool than an institutional lender like a bank.

A secured loan is one where the borrower pledges an asset as collateral for the loan. Easy way to think of this: your car loan. When you went to the dealership and financed the purchase of an automobile you "assigned" an interest in that car to the company that provided the money to pay the dealer. If you were to default on the loan, the company providing the financing has the right to seize your car and sell it to pay off the loan. The loan was "secured" by the car.

Unsecured loans are loans where you do not personally pledge any of your assets to obtain the money.

Collateral is a security or guarantee, an asset, pledged until such time as the loan is repaid. In the example I just used, the car is considered the "collateral" for the loan. In a business or real estate transaction the amount of the collateral determines how much the lender will offer as a loan amount.

A Personal Guarantee is your promise to repay the debts of the company in the event of a default by the business. If your business doesn't have enough assets to pay off the loans of the business, and you have made a personal guarantee, then the lender has the right to take your other assets to satisfy the debt. This can even include your personal home if you have equity in it.

 off the loan they're considering offering you. It is almost impossible to obtain financing for a start up business venture without a personal guarantee.

Ways to Raise Money

It is unusual for a first time entrepreneur to be able to completely fund their business without using some borrowed money. Here are some sources of that money that you have probably already thought of, and some you may not have. I'll be brief here, because there are many books written on this subject and business consultants who are experts at raising money. I just want to give you some basic ideas and vocabulary so you can better direct your search efforts.

Friends and Family. I hesitate to suggest you go to those in the whole world who know you best and ask them for money. They know you...and always seem to have long memories...particularly when it comes to money. So use your own judgment on this one.

What you might consider doing is offering a family member an equity position in your business in return for some or all of the money you need. Again, there are both pluses and minuses of this strategy. On the positive side you won't have to pay back some or all of the loan. If you have underestimated how long it takes to be profitable in the business an equity partner/family member is likely to be more patient than a banker. The negative side is that you've given up some percentage of control of your business, and to a family member. How much criticism of your business acumen do you really want to hear at the next family gathering?

Home equity loan. These loans used to be quite common and easy to get. That was when the bank could reasonably assume that the value of your home was going to increase every year. Since that is no longer the case, a home equity loan is far more difficult. If you have considerable equity and good credit, this can be the least expensive and longest term payback of any of your financing options. Remember, this loan is secured by your home. The mortgage company does not retain any interest in your business. In fact, it is probably better not to tell them that you're using the money to start a new business.

Venture Capital (VC). This is a type of private equity capital that is typically given in the early stages of a potentially high growth company. The investor is betting that your business idea grows quickly and can eventually become part of an Initial Public Offering or trade/sale of the company.

The typical VC investor is an institution or high net worth

individual. Their investment is normally cash for an equity stake in the company. Often there is a time constraint to a VC investment. That is, you have three years to take the company public or some other method of getting their money and return on investment back to them. If the company isn't "ready" for one of the VC exit strategies within their time table, you may be required to secure additional financing to reduce their participation or completely buy them out.

If you've ever watched "Shark Tank" on television, you are seeing a form of applying for funding with a Venture Capital investor. In reality the process is much more involved than making a 3 minute pitch and demonstrating your product or service. The type of questions asked by the Sharks on the program are indicative of what you'll hear from VC investors.

If your new business idea has enough potential. Venture Capitalists may be interested in it.

Your Landlord. Many commercial building owners and managers are facing higher than usual vacancy rates in their properties. It is typical in an economy like this to ask the landlord for tenant finish funds in return for a longer term lease. They may also be willing to give you several months free rent at the front end of the lease and/or pay for moving expenses to help you get your enterprise to their building.

Keep in mind that most commercial leases will require a personal guarantee and can be quite expensive to terminate early.

Credit Cards. Borrow the maximum cash available on your credit cards to finance your business. This was a common practice just a few years ago that has become more difficult. Credit card companies have tightened credit lines and monitor sudden jumps in the amount of credit outstanding quite closely.

There are some of the "prestige" cards that are specifically designed for small business owners. Both American Express and Diners Club, at the time of this writing, offer a special card program to their business owner clients. If you carry these cards it is worth investigating.

The negative side of financing business start up or growth with credit cards is that they typically carry a higher interest rate. The minimum monthly payment can be seductive, but this makes it way too easy to get upside down in cash flow quickly.

Inventory Suppliers. Do you buy a lot of raw material to be used in your business? Can you get your supplier to extend your credit terms? Being able to go from Cash on Delivery to 14 days for example, gives you a full two weeks to take the raw product, process and sell to your customer. This can be a significant help in many industries.

Make certain you pay the supplier on time. If you were to default and they refuse to sell to you, and there were not another ready source of product you could immediately access, you could be out of business in a matter of days.

Equipment Suppliers. Capital expenditures like equipment can often be financed for longer periods of time, even years depending on the equipment. Another thought is to lease the equipment instead of purchasing. This will minimize the upfront expense, but add a monthly cost to your business.

If your supplier does not have a leasing program in place, you might investigate a **3rd Party Leasing Company.** This company will come in and purchase the equipment on your behalf, then lease it back to you. They charge a premium for doing so, but it can help conserve your capital as your begin your business.

SBA Guarantees. The Small Business Administration is an agency of the Federal government. They have a couple of programs that guarantee a loan made to your business by a lender. An advantage of the SBA programs is that they will loan on a start up business.

A Partner. There is an old joke that says you should never be in a business partnership with someone unless you are willing to marry them. While that is an exaggeration, entering into a business partnership is not to be taken lightly. You are most likely going to be giving up both equity and some decision making authority to your partner. Are you willing to do this?

In a typical case, the person with the business idea or technical understanding of the business seeks a partner who can bring money to the table. The difference between this structure and the other investment scenarios we've talked about is the equity piece. Your partner will want a larger piece of the pie and for a longer time. If you have really designed a great business and in a couple of years it is worth a ton of money, are you going to resent having to share with your partner, especially if you've done most of the work?

I have been in several very productive partnerships in my career. Each time, when our business was done we had survived the stress of the partnership and remained friends. That is not always the case. My suggestion is that if you are considering forming a partnership that your partnership agreement includes very specific terms as to how the partnership is to be ended should one or both partners want out. There must be a mutual buy-out provision, as well as a plan for the surviving partner if one should die prematurely.

A partnership is one of the business structures that I would absolutely not attempt without having an attorney's input. Attorney's are trained to think about all the bad things that can happen, and will help you and your partner decide what to do if any of those things come to pass.

What is my opinion?

Spend the least amount possible to get your business idea to the point where you are actually selling to real customers. If you can test your idea without borrowing any money, then do it. If everything isn't "perfect" yet, that's OK, get selling.

There is a slang business expression, "boot strapping." I'm not sure where it started, I know in the early days of computers it meant hardwiring a computer to a preliminary program that was read before executing another instruction; a "boot strap."

For the entrepreneur I think it has more to do with the Old West saying "pulling up oneself by one's bootstraps" and it means doing as much as you can with what you have before taking on debt or partners.

Want my advice? That's it. Do everything that you can to test your idea in front of real prospects who you are asking to put their hard earned money on the table to buy what you are offering. If they say yes in sufficient quantities, then you know you have a good idea and will find it easy to get the money to build your idea out to a nice business.

If those real world customers say no, and you can't modify your offer to the point where they say yes, then that's an even more valuable lesson! Now you know that the idea isn't scalable to a business at this point, and you've saved yourself a lot of work, expense, and debt.

Let me express this lesson in a little different way. One of my best friends likes to gamble. I mean Las Vegas style table gambling. One of the lessons he is always sharing is that when you are "on a roll" you let your bets ride. When the cards or dice "seem to be favorable" then press your bets and just keep going. However, when the cards or dice "turn cold" and you begin to lose; that means it's time to get up and find a new table or just step away for a few minutes and regroup.

The people that get crushed at the casinos, he tells me, are the ones who can't recognize when it's time to get up and walk away.

I'm not a gambler, at least not that kind of gambling. But I understand how important it is to know when the market isn't ready for your business idea, or wants you to change it. The entrepreneur who recognizes this marketplace phenomenon and listens, adjusting his/her plans as the customers dictate, lives and thrives in their business. The business owner who insists that their idea is right and tries to swim upstream against the market gets overwhelmed by the current and spit up on the shoreline.

Don't get spit up on the shoreline!

Chapter 3

"Now that I've got texting, email,
Facebook, and Twitter, I'll never
have to talk with anyone
face-to-face again!"

Question #2: What Ongoing Overhead
Is Needed?

Once you have determined your budget for the initial investment in your business, the next important consideration is to calculate the day to day cost of operating your business once it's open. This will be a significant part of your business plan. In most cases an investor will ask you to calculate ongoing monthly expenses for at least the first 24 months of operation.

Here is a brief list of some of the items that may be a

part of your cost structure. This is by no means a complete list, but is just intended to get you thinking about what is will cost to be in business.

1. Cost of Goods—what is the cost of your inventory that you pay to suppliers?

2. Employee Costs—will you need employees? If so, how many, and for what number of hours each week? Remember, their salary or hourly wage is not the final cost. Estimate 30% above that total to calculate your final cost including all tax and government fees.

3. Variable costs—utilities for your place of business. Transportation, both cost of getting inventory to you as well as any cost of delivery to your customers. Office supplies. Printing. Etc.

4. Occupancy Cost—Rent, and don't forget common area maintenance fees if they are included in your lease.

5. Marketing Cost. How will people know you are in business and what you offer?

As you can see, there are a great many considerations beyond the initial cost of acquiring a business.

If you purchase a franchise, the franchisor will almost certainly have a specific accounting procedure and reporting system they require you to use. Their forms will take into consideration all of the expenses involved in running that particular business for you. This certainly makes your job easier, and is one of the reasons to consider investing in a franchise.

Have you thought about this....?

Another type of "overhead" that you may not have considered is your time. What is your time worth per hour? Are you going to be the primary manager of the business? What hours is your business going to be open? If you have an internet based business, how many hours a week are you going to devote to it? How long can you survive without paying yourself a salary if the company can't support you in the early going?

If you finance the launch of your business by taking on a partner, will both of you be physically working in the business? Does this mean that the business will need to support two "owner" salaries? If so, how soon will this need to happen?

If you have had a career in the corporate, government, or military world, are you prepared to work the hours that will be necessary as a business owner? Again, depending on the type of business you choose to go into, that can be 50 hours a week...or 60 hours a week...or more. What is the impact on your life, and your family, if you suddenly have that commitment?

What is my opinion?

In this case I have two opinions—or more accurately, an opinion for the entrepreneur who wants to create a full time business and another for the person seeking a second source of income.

Let me speak to the full time person first. You have a good idea that you want to put into a business. Or you've retired from the military or a "first career" and don't want to just "go fishing."

In the last chapter I encouraged you to test your ideas as fully as possible before making a large investment. This time my advice is very similar—keep your expenses as low as possible in the early going, sacrifice style for security. Use an executive suite instead of leasing your own office space. Work with a virtual assistant until you need a full time support person. Go to the big box office supply store for copies before leasing equipment.

Think big, but act small in the early going!

If you're looking to test a retail idea, look for a sublease of space. See if you can find a part of an existing store with a non-competing product you can set up in to test your idea. Get a booth at a trade show that is appropriate for your product and see how the public reacts to your offer.

Think big, but act small in the early going!

Have a product you want to develop and take to market? Get a couple of prototypes as inexpensively as possible and shop them around to potential retail outlets. Participate in a trade show. Put up a website describing your product with photos of the prototype and test various prices and offers. See if anyone is interested in buying. Only then, consider contracting for production of a real inventory.

Think big, but act small in the early going!

Let me give you a personal example. I started a mortgage company back in the early 1990's. My partner and I leased a 220 square foot executive office suite. It came with two desks, two chairs, and two telephones. There was a receptionist at the front who served all the tenants, and a conference room we could schedule when a client came to see us.

It was crowded in our little office. It was hard to hear when we were both on the phone at the same time. The only luxury we insisted on was having a coffee maker in our office so we didn't have to drink the swill out of the machine.

We stayed there for six months, then moved to a slightly larger executive suite with room for a third desk. That worked for another six months. We then moved to a nearby office building and leased 1000 square feet. This required a modest investment in used office furniture and a receptionist/assistant/and whatever else employee. We were really styling!

By our third year in business we had leased the entire floor in that building. The following year took another half floor, plus had offices in two other cities. By our fifth year we had over 50 employees, were licensed in 36 states, and generating over $3 million in revenue.

Did we visualize what our company would be in year five from day one? Yes, we dreamed of creating that kind of business. I believe the reason we were able to accomplish that is because we spent our first year in a crowded executive suite on an interior hallway with bad lighting.

Think big, but act small in the early going.

A business category to consider if you are looking for a new, full time business is a franchise. I'm going to talk about franchise opportunities extensively in chapter 6.

Now, what about the person who is not interested in creating a full time business, but just wants a second source of income. You want to create a little extra security, some additional money to put aside each month for retirement or a college fund for the kids or grandkids.

If this describes you, my first encouragement is to evaluate opportunities that can be managed from your home. A "home based business" will allow you to keep costs down and begin part time while keeping your primary source of income. This allows you to "test" the new business to make sure it is something that you can be successful at, and will enjoy working.

While it may seem obvious, the easiest path to profit is to have no additional fixed overhead and very low operating costs. This insures that even a small amount of sales at the start of your business gives you immediate profits.

Businesses that fall into the category of "home based" are often in the direct sales or network marketing area. While some people have had a bad experience themselves or with a family member who tried "one of those" businesses, I believe that a carefully chosen company in this category can provide an excellent opportunity for immediate part time income in today's marketplace. The fact that many of these companies also have a residual income component is another reason to consider affiliating with one of these opportunities.

Another "home based" business is that of "Affiliate Marketing." To be successful here you only need a place to work, computer, and a high speed internet connection.

In this new edition of Ten Vital Questions I have an extensive analysis of the network marketing and affiliate marketing business models and some criteria you should include in your evaluation of these opportunities. These discussions are in Part Two of the book.

Chapter 4

"To be successful, we have to treat customers like <u>family</u>."

"Real family or in-laws?"

Question #3: Does the Business Require You to Hire Employees or Inventory a Product to Resell?

In the last chapter we talked about some of the costs associated with starting your new business. Without doubt, the two biggest ongoing expenses of most any business are the costs of labor and product inventory. The more you can minimize these expenses, the greater your probability for success.

Let's look at each of these categories individually. First, employees.

Many of us have the idea that if we can hire "good people" that our business will require less of our time. A good idea, but difficult to put into practice. Consider some of the hidden costs associated with having a team of people in your business.

Training time, and the cost of materials to properly orient your new employee. Did you know that Starbucks sends a new barista to two weeks of training at a regional training center, then another week in the store they are going to work at, before they are qualified to represent the company with customers? That's just to make a cup of coffee! Can you afford this initial expense to make sure your staff is fully prepared to represent you and your business?

Turnover. Just when you have someone in a position where they are productive, they get an offer from another company and you have to begin again with a new person. Or you invest time and money training and they just quit for any number of other reasons.

Turmoil within your staff. If you've been a parent of more than one child, I'm sure you can remember many occasions when they didn't get along, and were quite vocal about it. And those are siblings who love each other! If you have more than one employee you can bet money that the same thing is going to happen. They'll get into squabbles with each other, and always at the least opportune time. Oh, and then they'll expect you to be the referee.

Theft. Truth is, not everyone is honest. If you have a staff of employees, at some time in the future you will experience a theft in your business. It may not be money. It could be pilfering inventory or inaccurately reporting payroll or not ringing up sales to their friends. There are many ways an employee can "beat the system." All of these cost you money.

Then there is the "indirect" cost of employees. As an employer you are required by law to provide a minimum bundle of tax/insurance benefits that total almost 8% in addition to what you are paying the employee. These include social security, Medicare, unemployment insurance, and workers compensation.

Here are some additional categories of compensation that are not required by law, but may become a "practical necessity" for your business if you want to keep good managers and employees on your team. These include:

Paid Leave

- ✓ Vacation
- ✓ Holidays
- ✓ Sick days
- ✓ Personal days

Supplemental Pay

- ✓ Overtime or premium pay
- ✓ Shift differentials
- ✓ Non-production related bonuses

Insurance

- ✓ Health
- ✓ Life
- ✓ Short term disability
- ✓ Long term disability

Retirement

- ✓ Defined-benefit pension contributions
- ✓ Defined-contribution pension plans

The US Bureau of Labor Statistics ECEC survey measures the average cost to employers wages, salary, and benefits per employee per hour worked. While there is occasionally a slight variance between years, for the purpose of calculation you would be safe to use a figure of 30% (that is actually a little lower than current statistics.) That means that for an employee that you are paying $10 per hour in wages, you as the employer will be paying an average of an additional $3 per hour for that employee. So a $1000 weekly payroll actually costs you $1300.

Much of the time a small business will not incur the pension and total benefit package listed above. However, it would be foolish to estimate any less than 20% above the cost of wages as you budget for employee costs.

Here's another consideration for a small business. In every case you will have employees that do multiple tasks as a normal part of their job. Where a big national company uses ten people, you have to get by with three or four. That kind of staffing works when everyone is healthy and shows up at work. That doesn't happen every week. In fact, the actual number of productive work days for the average employee is staggering. Here's the numbers:

261   work days (5/7 of 365 days in the year)
 (8)   government holidays
(14)   vacation for a seasoned employee
 (7)   average sick days per year
(10)   average training days per year

222 net actual productive work days

This number does not include the average days lost per employee if you have a maternity leave case during the year.

Scary but true! Over 15% of the work year is potentially lost. Again, in most small companies you can reduce the number of days away from work, but it would be foolish to assume that your team is always going to be at work as scheduled.

Inventory Considerations

Inventory is another huge expenditure. How many products will you stock? How much money will you have tied up in inventory sitting on the shelves? What do you do with products that don't sell in a timely manner? If your inventory is perishable, how do you insure selling it in time?

If you are in a retail business then your inventory will be the single largest item on your balance sheet. If you have a manufacturing company then the raw product and work in process when added together will be your largest asset.

If you are thinking about a business in one of these categories then inventory security becomes a major consideration. You will certainly have to have secure storage areas in your business space, and may need to hire security personnel.

An important metric related to inventory is "turnover." That is the number of times that your inventory sells out in a year. In almost every segment of specialty retail: gift, clothing, sporting goods, jewelry, shoes, books, music, electronics, appliances, furniture, and many more; the turnover rate has held steady for the past twenty-five years at less than 4 times.

This means that most of these stores are carrying at least three months of sales in their store at any given moment. This is not only a drain on the owners financial position, but also can reduce your ability to properly take care of your customers. What I mean by that is you cannot restock what is selling because you have too much of what is not selling.

I don't want to bog you down with a lot of extraneous

detail, but if you are considering any business opportunity where maintaining an inventory of any size is going to be a component, there are three other factors to be aware of. These are the SKU intensity, the reorder cycle time, and the nature of the inventory (either consumable or discretionary.) Let's briefly define each of these.

SKU intensity is usually the most critical factor in managing your inventory. What it means is how many Stock Keeping Units (SKU's) you have per item. If you're in the gift business you might only have one SKU per item if they are unique or single size pieces. If you expect to sell twelve in a month you may only need to have twelve on hand.

What if you're in a clothing business where you carry four sizes of an item (S, M, L, and XL) and three colors (red, blue, and green). If you expect to sell twelve pieces in a month you'd have to stock in your inventory 144 units! Theoretically, you would have to assume that all twelve customers would want the same color and size, and be prepared in all combinations of size and color.

In the real world you wouldn't (couldn't!) manage an inventory this way. You would use your sales history and industry averages to estimate the percentage of your customers in each size, then make a similar determination as to color preference between the three choices. Yes, you'd still have a few customers who could not find what they wanted, but with proper SKU management you can minimize this dissatisfaction.

Reorder cycle time is simply how long it takes to get fresh inventory into your store once you place your order with a supplier. The longer the cycle time the greater quantity of inventory you'd have to maintain. A well managed retail operation establishes what is called a "model stock." This is the desired inventory level of each item based on SKU analysis and cycle time.

The third factor is the nature of the inventory. Some inventory items are purchased every day by customers, others more infrequently. A typical buyer will purchase several pairs of slacks in a year, a tube of toothpaste every month, and bananas weekly. However, they would probably only purchase a new television set every three or four years.

Products that have a higher purchase frequency rate almost always have a lower replacement cost. Low purchase frequency equals higher price. These lower purchase frequency items are also referred to as "deliberation" merchandise because the consumer will often take time and do some research before purchase. Often more than one trip to the store is required before making a decision.

The key to ensure your profitability if you carry a lot of these "deliberation" items, or any slower moving pieces of your inventory, is to make certain that you have a higher margin of profit. Essentially, you have to factor in how long the item is going to "rent" space on your shelf or sales floor, and make sure there is adequate profit to "pay the rent."

I've spent a lot of time describing things you'll want to be aware of regarding inventory because almost any small business, even home based, will have some level of inventory. Frequently the true cost and impact of maintaining products for sale is not taken into consideration by someone planning their business.

What is my opinion?

My first business where I was an equity partner was a chain of restaurants. We started from zero and over a period of four years created a company with sixteen locations, over 1800 employees in total, and tens of thousands of dollars of perishable inventory on hand at any given moment.

You may not have thought about it this way, but a restaurant is really a small manufacturing company. Raw product comes in the back door each day (inventory). The kitchen staff converts that raw food into the finished plates that are on the menu (manufactures it). The marketing staff (waiters and waitresses), go out to the customers (guests in the dining room) and take their orders. The manager in the dining room goes around to the tables and asks the guests how their meal is (market research).

Think about that next time you stop by Burger King!

My partners and I were working 70 hours a week to try and stay in front of the wave that our company had become. The constant turnover of employees and managers was costing us thousands of dollars and valuable time. Our menu required a high percentage of fresh produce and dairy products—all perishable in just a day or two.

While we had a successful business, we had no life! And given how hard we were working and our financial liability, the return on investment was just not that great. Truthfully, I was relieved when we were able to sell this company.

I share that early experience because it dramatically affected how I have looked at business opportunities in the thirty years since. I have always looked for a way to automate and systematize a business to minimize the number of staff required. Since that restaurant company, I have never, not once, gotten involved in a business that necessitated the stocking of perishable inventory.

I advise my clients to look for the ideal business: one that does not require employees, or very few employees, to get the company started; or the stocking of inventory. While that sounds unrealistic, such businesses do exist, particularly since the advent of the internet.

Chapter 5

"To be successful in business, you need a creative environment, creative people,

and creative accounting."

Question #4: Do You Have To Do Any Invoicing, Collections, or Carry Any Accounts Receivable?

An important consideration for any business owner is how much of the accounting work will you have to do as a part of your day to day management of the enterprise? Here are some specific tasks:

1. Invoicing. Will you be billing customers for products or services you have already provided? If so, what sort of payment terms will you be asking for? That is, how quickly do you expect your customers to pay you for their purchases? What accounting software system will you implement to help you manage this activity?

2. Accounts receivable. If you are selling business to business, it is likely that you will have to wait for a period of time to actually collect your money. In a difficult economy like we are now experiencing, many of your customers might not be able to pay you on time...or at all.

Also realize that if you accept credit cards there is often a two to five day time lag between when you upload your sales activity and when the credit card company makes a deposit into your account. If you're operating on a tight cash flow, as many new businesses are, this can be problematic.

3. Collections. What will you do with delinquent accounts? How will you attempt to collect what is owed to you while still maintaining the relationship with the customer? At what point do you consult with your attorney?

4. Accounts payable. We've already discussed the numerous expense categories that can be a part of your

new business. Someone has to pay those bills every week or month.

5. Daily Sales Reconciliation. If you use any type of point of sales system in your business, each day there is a balancing function that must be done. This can be as simple as matching the total sales to the amount of cash and credit card transaction slips you have at the end of the day. If your point of sales system also tracks item sales this data must be processed for analysis. Bank deposits have to be prepared and taken to the bank or given to an armed pick up service.

6. Payroll processing. If you have employees you will also have two or more pay periods each month. That means someone has to total all of the hours worked for each staff member, calculate their earnings, accurately report taxes and other deductions, and generate a pay check. There are also monthly, quarterly, and annual reporting and deposit requirements to be completed.

Who is going to handle all of this in your business?

The simple answer to the accounting challenge of a small business is that you can just have a outside contract book keeper handle all the accounting tasks for your company and retain one of the payroll processing companies to deal with those functions. Then you have a CPA firm review their work and prepare your management reports each month.

Sounds easy right? It can be. It can also be expensive, and leaves you vulnerable to the competence of the book keeper. Whether you have an "in house" employee who processes all of your accounting functions, or contract with another service provider, you as the owner are ultimately responsible for the accuracy of all records and filings with government entities.

A good rule to follow is this: as a business owner you can delegate, but never abdicate. What I mean by that is you will have to assign responsibilities to people on your team—you can't do everything. But you can never completely take yourself out of the loop, especially in the accounting for your business. Far too many of my clients and business associates have been shocked to find that their accounting person, through ignorance or intent, performed in a way that caused them great harm and expense.

Management Reports

There are three significant financial management reports that you as a business owner must have at hand to review at least monthly. These tools give you a snapshot of the overall financial health and performance of your enterprise.

A word of advice concerning these reports. Don't just glance at the bottom line and assume if it "looks OK" that your business is healthy. Each of these reports individually has important data for you to absorb. But it is in their collective assembling of financial information, and the careful analysis and correct interpretation of that data, that you will gain valuable insight into how to protect and grow your company.

The three reports are: the profit and loss statement, the balance sheet, and the cash flow statement. I want to briefly describe each, and suggest how you should use them synergistically to manage your business.

Profit and Loss Statement—this is a historical record, sometimes called an Income Statement. It shows you how much you've made in sales, how much you've spent, and what your net income is over a specific period of time. The time period could be a week, month, quarter, or year. Most business owners look at this data monthly, although in the early months of your enterprise a weekly snapshot could be valuable.

P&L data is often expressed as both a dollar amount and a percentage of sales. This is valuable since you will quickly establish cost percentage benchmarks for your business. If you know that any new product you consider offering your customers must carry a 30% or less cost of goods to fit into your business model, then it becomes simple arithmetic to evaluate what the necessary selling price of a potential new item must be. If that is beyond the market, you know you probably can't bring it into stock.

A P&L tells you whether or not you're making money, and how much you are either making or losing. If structured properly, this report can also show you which products and services are selling the best, and where you are spending too much on expenses.

A common mistake that I see new business owners make is confusing percentages with dollars. Here's what I mean. You look at the P&L and notice that it says your cost of goods is only 35%. "Great," you say to yourself, "I budgeted 38%." Since you are 3% ahead of where you thought you'd be, there is a temptation to assume you have more money to spend elsewhere. Hold on for a second. Can you take a percentage to the bank? Or pay your utility bill with one? Of course not! The P&L is a good summary of operational effectiveness. It must be evaluated along with your other financial reports to get a completely accurate understanding of your business health at that moment.

Balance Sheet—this is a snapshot of your company's financial health. It provides a summary of your assets, liabilities, and net worth. This report is sometimes called the "statement of financial condition" and, in essence tells you what you own and what you owe. The asset side of the report (it's often presented in a two column format) will show all the resources that your business controls. These include cash, equipment, real estate, furniture, and accounts receivable. The liabilities of your company are what you owe to others: accounts payable, taxes, payroll, loans, etc. Your Net Worth (or Equity) is what is left over when you subtract your liabilities from your assets.

Cash Flow Statement—perhaps the most important for a small business owner. This captures how cash has flowed in and out of your company over a specific period of time. An easy way to think of this report is like the ledger in your checkbook, which shows deposits you make, checks you write, and the remaining balance.

I suggest this is the most important of the three reports for you because the P&L might indicate that you are profitable, but you may not be generating any cash. How can that be? Easy. Your sales may be growing rapidly as billings increase to new customers, but those customers are slow to pay—so you have good looking sales but no cash coming in. Another way is that you are building up inventory in anticipation of a busy season or heavily advertised upcoming sale. You have an "asset" in the inventory without the accompanying sales having occurred yet. The Cash Flow Statement will indicate this temporary imbalance.

Why is this data so valuable? Using either of the all too normal examples in the previous paragraph, you are temporarily a little short on cash. What if you have a payroll due on Friday? You know that your employees cash or deposit their checks almost immediately. If you are regularly monitoring your cash flow you can be alerted to this in time to make plans to avoid a problem.

What report format to choose for your business? Any accounting package that you use is going to have a series of reports that you can customize for your specific operation. If you are going to use a book keeping service and/or CPA firm they will be able to help you design reports that will be meaningful tools.

That's the most important consideration. Having analysis tools that provide an accurate analysis of the relevant metrics for your business.

What is My Opinion?

The most important activity that any business owner does is the marketing of the business. Anything else that takes your time is a hidden expense of the business. Spending your time dealing with the accounting for the business can be a distraction that keeps you from doing the things that will make you successful. To the extent that you can minimize accounting responsibility and expense, you should do so.

I encourage you not to get involved with any business where you have to carry a high percent of your sales in accounts receivable or be involved with collecting for your product or service. Especially in the early days, difficulty in collecting accounts receivable alone could put you out of business.

If internet sales are going to be a part of your business plan, a good relationship with your merchant account provider will help you manage your cash flow. A surprising number of large and well established businesses now accept PayPal, the "credit card" of Ebay. That is something you should investigate for your business as many people who do not have major credit cards do have a Pay Pal account and use it often.

Remember, the goal of this book is to challenge you to identify opportunities that are low risk with a high probability of success. You must reduce or eliminate any activity that takes you away from strategic planning and marketing.

Gordon Van Wechel

Chapter 6

"Okay, I put everything in priority
order. I have 192 "A's, 11 "B's, and
1 "C". Now what?"

Question #5: Does The Business Have Proven Systems For You To Follow?

Have you ever visited a cave or underground cavern at a state or national park? Usually there is a park ranger who leads a group down into the cave, describing the geology and what you are looking at. Eventually you'll come to an underground grotto where, with proper warning to stand completely still, the ranger turns out all the lights and you're in total—and I mean total—

darkness. After a brief time the ranger will strike a match, demonstrating how a very small amount of light can penetrate all that inky blackness. There's lots of "oohs" and "aahs," and a couple of frightened children, but all in all it's a fun experience.

If you've never been in a business of your own before, visualize that pitch black underground cavern as the environment you're walking into. You may have a lot of desire, a high energy level, and even be adequately capitalized. But without even the small amount of light from a match to give you direction, you will most likely fall off the path into a deep hole and be lost.

In Chapter One I talked about the importance of a comprehensive business plan. Equally vital is a marketing plan. If you utilize one of the business planning software programs or checklists available on line or in books, all will include a "marketing" section in their business plan. Call me biased...but that is not enough. To my way of thinking, your marketing plan is the single most important component in your business plan.

A primary reason that people choose to invest in a franchise opportunity is because others have already proven that the business idea works and can be profitable. As a franchisee you will be given operating manuals that detail all of the steps you'll need to take before you open your doors, and after you are up and running. Many franchise companies require their new owners to attend a training program that can last a week or more.

That is really what your franchise fee is paying for. If you have never owned your own business it can be a smart decision to invest in a proven system. However, what I have read in numerous franchise agreements that I've reviewed for clients is a strong emphasis on proven "operating systems;" but very little comment on how the new franchisee is going to get customers in the door, not much of a "marketing system."

One more related thought. I would strongly encourage you not to get involved in a business opportunity that required extensive training for or skills in an area that you are completely unfamiliar with. Even a proven franchise opportunity cannot overcome a steep learning curve in many cases. Every industry, and every business, has its own vocabulary and customs. You're going to be facing numerous challenges just being a new business owner. Don't further complicate the equation by choosing a business type that you are totally new to.

The most important system you should look for is one that gets you sales—we often refer to this as a "sales funnel." Many opportunities will give a tremendous amount of detail about the activities of running your new business, but not tell you how to market your business. If there is not a very specific, step by step program in place to teach you how to best promote your new business, then I would be unwilling to invest my time or money.

The sales funnel for your new business needs to be more than a signage package and some ad slicks. You want a very specific marketing plan designed to identify and penetrate the various markets that your product/service is targeting. There is an important concept in marketing that says, "if everyone is your customer, then no one is your customer." What that means is that you must be able to target a group of potential buyers in a focused way and bring them into a relationship with you and your business if you are going to enjoy long term success. Anything short of this and you increase your risk!

We call this "niche marketing" and I'm going to talk more about this concept in chapter nine. For now, I want to go into more depth on what should be included in your marketing plan.

By now you know my bias: marketing is the single most important activity that a business owner does. Everything that distracts you from this primary function is an expense! As I said, I believe that the marketing plan is the most important part of your total business plan. Here are some facts that I suggest you include in your plan:

1. Is there a market for your product/service? Prove it.

The first component of your marketing plan is a Market Analysis. You've introduced your business idea and described your product(s) or service in the Executive Summary part of your business plan. The Market Analysis is your opportunity to demonstrate that someone out there needs you...that you are filling a market void. That doesn't mean that you are the only player in the market—that almost never happens. What you need to demonstrate is that you have a clear understanding of the market you are entering. Who the other players are, and what they offer.

Early in your marketing plan you want to share your Unique Selling Proposition. I mentioned this term earlier in the book, now let me define it. Your USP is the very essence of what you are offering. Your USP needs to be so compelling that it can be used as a headline that sells your product or service. Here are some examples of excellent USP statements. I bet you know the companies:

"Pizza delivered in 30 minutes or it's free!"

"The nighttime, coughing, achy, sniffling, stuffy head,

fever, so you can rest medicine."

"When it absolutely, positively, has to be there over night."

Did you recognize them? Dominos, Nyquil, and Federal Express?

You don't have to write an award winning headline that can be used in a national television commercial. You do want to carefully think about exactly what your business is and be able to reduce it to a succinct statement of the benefits you offer. The key word that I just wrote is BENEFITS.

I'm going to spend a couple of paragraphs talking about this distinction because it is a common mistake; that is, the difference between a feature and a benefit. A feature is a characteristic about your product. The benefit is what's in it for the customer. Sales people, marketing materials, even national television campaigns will proudly tout their products features but never connect that feature to what is it's real value to the customer. How does that feature meet the need of the prospect? The better you can articulate this clear value to the customer the faster you will grab market share for your product or service.

Let me give you some examples of what I mean.

✓ The telephone salesperson tells the customer, "this cell phone has a touch sensitive lighted dial," and then stops talking. The lighted dial is a feature. Probably a good one, but without sharing with the customer a direct benefit to him or her, the salesperson has just made a meaningless statement.

Here's another way to phrase it as a benefit, "you know how sometimes you need to use your phone at night, or you reach for it when you're riding in the car after dark? Well this model has a touch sensitive lighted dial so you can immediately use it to send a text or check something out online."

See the difference? Let's try another.

✓ You are shopping for a car and the salesperson tells you, "this model has a rear view camera." That's a feature. What's the benefit? Well, there could be several. Here's one, "I know you said you live on a street with lots of families so your kids have plenty of playmates. This model we're looking at has a rear view camera and warning sensor system. This means you can have confidence that when you're backing up the car will let you know if someone small is in your path. This model could help you avoid a terrible tragedy."

That kind of benefit statement is clear and graphically speaks to the prospect in a way that is important for them. One more.

✓ "Our store is well lighted and clean, with wide aisles." Feature! If that is all you tell someone, it would be easy to say, "so what?" Now, stated as a benefit: "we set up our store with wider than normal aisles, and strive to keep it clean and have more lighting in place so that you can easily find exactly what you're looking for and not be crowded while you shop."

The lesson I'm trying to convey is to be sure to state your USP as a benefit to your prospective customer. Do this with each aspect of your marketing, stress the benefit to the customer and not the product features, and you will build a loyal following of people who trust you and come back again and again.

1a. A tip for business plan presentation.

Plan to include graphics in your market analysis. These might include a chart of the population age by gender in your area highlighting the part of the population you are targeting with your business. Another piece of data that lends itself well to a graphic presentation is the geographical proximity to your anticipated location of your competitors. Any type of visual that enables your reader to improve their conceptual understanding of why you're excited about this opportunity is in your favor.   Photos, maps, product shots, architects renderings and space plan—all add to the strength of your marketing plan.

2. SWOT Analysis

This is an acronym that stands for: strengths, weaknesses, opportunities, and threats.   This is your opportunity to candidly address each of these topics for your potential investor as well as yourself. This does not have to be a long narrative of each. In fact, bullet points are best. You want to demonstrate that you've carefully analyzed every aspect of the business environment that you are planning to enter. In part two of this book is a chapter titled "Advanced Analysis." In it I talk in greater depth about the SWOT technique.

3. Competitive Analysis (more on this subject in Chapter 8)

Who is your direct competition? What do they do well? How close are they physically to where you plan to have your facility? Is their pricing higher, the same as, or lower than you anticipate for your products? Do they have more or less product availability? How do they market their business?

You get the idea I'm sure. A thorough understanding of the business people that you will be marketing against will enable you to design a better marketing strategy. Again, I'm going to refer you to the Advance Analysis chapter in part two for a more thorough discussion of best practices for completing a competitive analysis.

4. Marketing Strategy

Finally, we get to the good part!

After describing your competition, tell us why you are different and presumably better. What will you do to attract loyal customers that is not being done by these other business owners? Longer hours? Highly trained staff? More products available? Or a superior mix of products? Effective use of the internet? Local celebrities helping you advertise? Home delivery? A great returns policy? Anonymously turning your closest competitor into the IRS as a tax evader? (OK, I'm not really recommending that, just checking to see if you're paying attention.)

Here are the two "bottom line" questions: what is it about your USP that will attract customers and make your business a success? How are you going to let these potential customers know about your USP?

When you can thoroughly answer these two questions

then you have the foundation of a marketing strategy that you can systemize to grow your company.

What is my opinion?

I think I've already made my bias clear on this one. If you are looking at investing in a business, becoming a franchisee, or joining a direct selling company; and there is not a clear, well defined marketing plan for you to follow then don't buy it. If your goal is to start your own business from scratch, then focus your attention on a thorough understanding of your marketplace. After you really know what you're getting into, develop a comprehensive strategy for dominating that market. Don't settle for being a player hoping for a share and struggling over price competition. Go into business with the intention of being the premier player—the one every competitor is watching.

Gordon Van Wechel

Chapter 7

"Next time, make sure we have their money
before you get bright idea of showing
what our product can do."

Question #6: What is the Demand for Your Product/Service?

For a fifteen year period I travelled several times a year to countries in Central Asia and Africa teaching business start up strategies for several non-government organizations. We would help local entrepreneurs develop a business plan and seek financing through a loan fund developed specifically for this purpose. It was quite common when we had the first meeting with these potential business owners for them to be quite excited about their business idea. When I would ask them to demonstrate what their market was—who would be buying their product or service—most of the time they had not considered this.

I find the same is true here in the US. Many people believe they have a great idea for a business, or they have an interest they are passionate about that they think would convert easily to a business. Unfortunately they never investigate the potential marketplace for their idea, and fail.

Here is the vital question: is the product or service you are considering in huge demand by a large market of people? At least as important, do these people have money and are they willing to buy? It is even better if your market includes both business and retail consumers.

I often hear people talk about their business idea in terms of how it's "new" or "different." The truth, in my experience, is that something that is really unique takes a long time to create market momentum and acceptance...longer than most people have the cash flow to wait for. You are far better to go into a proven market and do an excellent job of service combined with creating the proper sales funnels and capturing your share of the existing business.

It probably has something to do with my age, but I find myself talking with a lot of potential business owners who are in their 50's. Many have 30 years with a company or government agency and can choose to retire with a pretty comfortable lifestyle. They are looking carefully at "second career" opportunities that have an entrepreneurial bent. After being a part of "the system" for so long, they want to flex a little and be in control of their business and destiny. But not without some serious concerns.

A person doesn't get to that point in life without remembering some significant turmoil in the markets. Many remember the first time OPEC decided to withhold oil production and the resulting chaos in America. Sitting in gas lines for two or more hours, the cost of almost everything in the grocery store dramatically increasing, a national feeling of powerlessness. Perhaps more than any other event this first oil crisis demonstrated that we were living in an international economy that wasn't afraid of the US anymore.

That was just the beginning. They also recall several real estate boom and bust cycles, interest rates as high as 18%, several wars, currency instability, unemployment— it's no wonder that the decision to start a business is fraught with peril for this generation. The underlying question is, "can I develop a business that has the capability of withstanding market turmoil? Is it possible to be recession proof?"

The answer is a solid yes. The fact is that people have created successful business models in every economic climate. There are those who would tell you that disorder and instability offer even more opportunity to the shrewd entrepreneur. So what do these people know that we can learn?

I think there are four business principles that you must consider if you're going to create a recession proof business. These four take into account the demographics of a society and the psychology of consumers who have less spendable income but still want to feel good about themselves. The four principles reflect a clear understanding of the kinds of products and services that should be offered in a difficult economic climate. Finally, they mandate that the entrepreneur carefully analyze how to multiply their working effectiveness. Here they are:

1. You must have **a huge and expanding market.** I said this earlier, and it is perhaps the most important consideration. You must choose a product or service that is in a market sector that is both huge and expanding. If expansion is slowed by economic trends, but the overall size of the market is still "huge" you can still do well. What is huge? Obviously it's industry dependent, but huge can refer to both the dollar volume

that is traded as well as the number of consumers within the market place.

It is not just enough to have a huge market, that market also needs to exist in your specific area. Several years ago I took a team of business people to China. While there we had many meals with the local business and county leaders. Every meal included the local delicacy, chicken feet; whether pickled or fried we knew before sitting down at the table that there would be a platter of feet.

After several days of this one of our team members started talking about the number of chicken farms and processing plants that were in his area (he was from Arkansas) and how he just knew that they were throwing away the feet. He was getting more and more excited about "capturing the chicken feet" market and how much he could make until another member of the team asked just how many American restaurants he thought were ready to put chicken feet on the menu? Or grocery stores felt a burning desire to allocate their refrigerated case space to this new product? It was obvious to us all that the answer was about zero!

We had a good laugh at our friend's expense for the rest of the trip. But how many times do you see someone open a business that is incongruous to that part of town or regional area?

2. You must have **a unique and consumable product or service.** A key to surviving, even thriving during a recessionary time, is selling a product that customers want to have, but they use it up regularly and need to come buy more. Often these are products or services without a lot of glamour. They might have a small price, but it really doesn't matter if it's being consumed regularly and quickly by a lot of people.

Remember how rapidly markets change in our wired world. It is not enough to be unique and consumable today, you have to be thinking twelve to twenty-four months ahead. More important, you have to be willing to flex with market demands, even changing your core business if that is what your customers are telling you they want. Want a quick example of a company that didn't do this? Kodak. After 100 years of market leadership, a long time membership in the exclusive Dow Jones 30, worldwide brand recognition; in the space of five years Kodak became a footnote. Too little and far too late.

3. Market timing! The **importance of getting front of large trends** cannot be over stated. It's the "rising tide floating all boats" phenomenon once again. You want to evaluate which industries are expanding or about to expand. A corollary to this is assessing the impact of changing social habits. At the time I'm writing this, June

of 2014, over 40% of all Google searches are originated from a mobile device. Just two years ago it was less than 15%. Four years ago, 0%.

Stop and think about how many brick and mortar companies have been put out of business in the last two years as the world has become confident in the safety of buying through the internet. Did those companies have to fail? Absolutely not! What is so interesting about the business environment we are living is that by properly leveraging the power of the internet and the global delivery system provided by UPS and FedEx, an entrepreneur can now run a very successful international business out of their garage!

Thomas Friedman wrote a book a couple of years ago called "The World Is Flat" in which he described a truly global economy that had already affected how the large international companies conducted their business. He predicted this trend would soon percolate down to the small entrepreneur. He was right, and that day is here.

4. The **importance of time leverage.** This is more than just striving to get more done in your working hours, it is also about empowering others. Look at business opportunities that encourage synergistic relationships. There is a significant difference in wealth creation between attempting to do everything yourself and training and empowering others to be able to work

along with you.

I'm not just talking about hiring employees and "leveraging" your time with their efforts. That is one way to achieve leverage, but with a lot of associated headaches. Another is working with independent agents. A good example of this model is a real estate broker who provides an office and business tools that are available to the agents who agree to share a part of their sales commissions in return for this service.

Direct selling and network marketing organizations are another example of the concept of time leverage. You invest your time and expertise into a person in your organization and help them become independent. They then duplicate that behavior with someone they know. You continue to benefit from the efforts of many while still doing the same work yourself.

What is my opinion?

I like being a small fish in a really big pond! I'm comfortable relying on my skills as a marketer to create a share of that larger pool of business. I know there is an image in the mind of many first time entrepreneurs that includes phrases like, "new and unique," or "rugged individualist" that have a real allure. You want to be in business to "pave your own way" and all that.

Trust me when I tell you that it is just too much work to create a market out of your idea, no matter how good the idea is. Since we really do now live in a worldwide economy, carving a small piece of that total volume of business that will allow you to live the lifestyle you want has become much easier.

Early adaptors work really hard. Those who come in at the start of the second phase, the "momentum" period, glean the wisdom of those who blazed the path but put themselves in front of the trend. These are the people who create a cash flow while they are in business, and a salable asset for when they want to stop.

Look for a business where there is a huge market, where you can sell to both business customers (B to B) and consumer customers (B to C). Then, identify one that is going into a momentum phase. That combination is not easy to find, but it's a homerun if you do!

Gordon Van Wechel

Chapter 8

"This Venn diagram tells us nothing,
but it's so cute!"

Question #7: How Much Competition Is There?

In the last chapter I suggested not being the first person into a market. In this chapter I want to look realistically at competition and how it affects your business idea.

There are a couple of ways to look at competition. First, what is the overall size of the market? This is a macro view of all the companies that sell the same or a similar product or service in the geographical area that you are planning to do business in. If you are planning to open a sandwich shop, for example, the first question is how many restaurants are in your area? Then, how many of them are sandwich shops, and how close are these shops to where you want to locate? When accompanied by other variables...population of the area, near a college, etc; you have a realistic picture of the marketing challenge you'll face getting customers.

If you are thinking about an internet based business, obviously the potential market goes beyond your immediate geographical area. The analysis is the same except that geographical location and proximity are analyzed by looking at how your competitors page rank on Google.

A side note before we begin. I will occasionally be reviewing a business plan with a client and read their competitive analysis. In so many words they will express the opinion that their idea is so innovative that they will have no competition. Big mistake! Every business has competition, and allowing your enthusiasm for your idea to delude you into believing that you won't is a potentially fatal error. Even if by some strange quirk you should be the first into your market with an idea, you can be 100% certain that your business will be copied quickly by someone who thinks they can do it better.

So just begin by recognizing the truth that you will have competition. Given that fact, let me suggest four criteria that you consider as you study the competitive environment that you are thinking about entering.

1. Defining Your Competitors. The first step is to identify your universe of competitors. Immediately this presents a challenge of definition. Is your competitor limited to a company that offers products or services that largely mirror those offered by your own company? What about companies that only offer one or two products/services that compete with your company's offerings? You have to decide what level of competition is material to your business.

Here's an example. You open a frozen yogurt store in a popular retail area with a lot of foot traffic. You're the only frozen yogurt in the area and enjoy a nice business. Then you notice that customers coming out of the deli across the street are carrying cups of frozen yogurt. Apparently the deli owner has purchased a single yogurt machine and is offering a new dessert to his patrons. Is that competition? Technically, it's not a new yogurt shop that has opened. Yet it is certainly reasonable to believe that in the past some of his customers have enjoyed their sandwich then walked over to your shop for dessert; and now they won't. How do you measure the impact on your business? How do you position your business to fight this intrusion into your market share?

Another market analysis challenge that small business owners must do is to scan the horizon for potential as well as current competitors. Just a few years ago Blockbuster owned the video rental business nationwide. Unfortunately, they didn't take seriously how the internet would change consumer shopping preferences and are now out of business. We live in a worldwide economy where an internet connection and a Pay Pal account can empower any consumer to be a citizen of the world. Are you competing at that level...or could your next door neighbor be buying exactly what you sell from a vendor on the other side of the country...or the world?

2. Analyzing Your Competitors Strengths And Weaknesses. Once you've identified who your competitors are, you can begin the process of identifying the strengths and weaknesses of those competitors.

The danger here for the small business owner is to place too much weight on the quality of the product or service they offer (or plan to offer, in the case of new business). This may be a comforting thought, but it reflects a fundamental misunderstanding of how business works. Customers don't always buy based just on the objective features of your product or service. The reality is that customer preferences also include price, service, location, convenience, the aesthetics of your space, attitude of your staff, and more.

What are some easy and inexpensive ways to analyze your competition? Go visit those that are in your immediate area. What is your experience as a customer? Ask a question and learn how the staff handles your inquiry. Buy something, then try to return it a day later and see how you are treated.

Look at their marketing materials. Do they run ads in the newspaper or local magazines? Is there a company brochure or catalogue? Web site? What do they say about their business to the public? What is their emphasis—product, service, shopping experience, location, unique inventory? What do they believe their customer's needs and priorities are as reflected in how they advertise their company. What benefits (not features!) do they offer?

Here's a fact that is true no matter what business or market segment you choose to compete in: over time, companies with financial resources, highly motivated or creative personnel, and other operational assets will prove to be tough, enduring competition that you'll need to take seriously. Investing time in advanced study will help you be in a better position to grab market share and insure your survival.

3. Analyzing Customer Needs and Wants

Learning about customer needs and wants is an important part of competitive analysis that is typically overlooked by the new business owner. Customer priorities should be your business's priorities. As an owner you also must take care that you don't limit your analysis to priorities that are already recognized in your market. New product development and new innovations in service are a natural part of the evolutionary cycle in any industry. Business owners and managers need to study and anticipate future customer needs and wants as well those needs and wants that are currently being addressed.

4. Studying Barriers to Entry. That's a "business speak" way of asking if there are challenges to someone who tries to come into your business category in the future that you have already overcome. These can become a competitive advantage for you. Here are several common barriers to entry for new competition:

- ✓ Patents. These provide some protection for new products or processes
- ✓ High start-up costs in many cases this barrier is the most daunting one for small businesses
- ✓ Knowledge. A lack of technical, manufacturing, marketing, or engineering expertise can all be a significant obstacle to successful market entry

✓ Market saturation. It is more difficult to carve out a niche in a crowded market than it is to establish a presence in a market marked by relatively light competition

What Is My Opinion?

As an owner, if you find yourself in a position where you are on the right side of one or more of these barriers, realize that it is going to be a short term advantage. Realistically, few barriers to entry last very long, particularly in newer industries. Even patents and trademarks do not provide nearly as much protection as is generally assumed. You'll need to be realistic in your projections about the period of time you can enjoy the market advantage provided by these barriers.

The purpose of competitive analysis exercises is to be certain you are aware of the competitive environment you are getting into. Competition can be a help in that it establishes the existence of a marketplace for you to enter. Of course the ideal situation is to discover a large market with almost no competition (if you find such a combination, please call me right away and I'll partner with you!) The reality is that every market is going to have competition. Know who they are and what they do well, create your business so that you are better, then market that difference.

Gordon Van Wechel

Chapter 9

"Our eggs are all in one basket,
no milk has been spilt, and
we have plenty of dough."

Question #8: Are There Niches to Market To?

A "niche" when we talk about marketing is a smaller group, a subset, of the entire marketplace. Said another way, a niche market is a focused, targetable portion of a market. By definition, then, a business that focuses on a niche market is addressing a need for a product or service that is not being addressed by mainstream providers. Think of a niche market as a narrowly defined group of potential customers.

This is an extremely important concept for the new business owner to grasp quickly. In fact, as you are evaluating business opportunities you will want to investigate how to define potential niche customer groups and include this strategy in your business plan.

For example, let's say you have just acquired a software product for managing a professional office environment. It works equally well in medical, dental, veterinary, consulting and legal practices. If you attempt to market to all of those separate groups with a single marketing campaign, most of the recipients will not "feel" as if you are talking to their profession, take your offer seriously, and buy your product.

The solution is to create a marketing funnel that targets each "niche" group individually, with specific marketing pieces focused on the needs and vocabulary of each profession. Don't design an ad that says, "9 out of 10 Doctors and Dentists Agree...." Make it two ads: "9 out of 10 Doctors agree...." Then, "9 out of 10 Dentists Agree...." That makes each doctor, dentist, lawyer, or consultant feel as though you've designed a product specific for their industry, and they are much more likely to look at incorporating it into their business. You have successfully "niched" your product.

Why should you bother to establish a niche market? Because of the great advantage of being alone there. Other small businesses may not be aware of your particular niche market, and large businesses won't want to bother with it.

I have talked with numerous business owners who fear this concept. They believe that they could be narrowing their potential sales and losing profit. The truth is, a niche market strategy gives your business power. A niche market allows you to define who you are marketing to. That knowledge enables you to better allocate your marketing energy and dollars.

A niche does not have to be a business category. Demographic niches are powerful to market to. For example, stay at home moms, retired couples, young adults at college. Each of these specialty markets can provide an excellent source of business, if correctly marketed to.

The trick to capitalizing on a niche market is to find or develop a market niche that has customers who are accessible, that is growing fast enough, and that is not already owned by one established vendor in your market area. Here are four basic concepts for niche marketing success to think about as you work to identify the best business opportunity for you.

1. A unique product or service.

If you're going to master a niche market, you need to have a unique product or service. Ideally, you want to be the only one selling what you're selling in your area.

The trick to coming up with such a product or service is to look on the fringes for unmet needs. Here is an example I recently ran across. I am a bonsai enthusiast, and belong to my local bonsai club. This is one of many, many clubs across the country. I don't know how many members are active in these clubs, but certainly several thousand. Bonsai is not a cheap hobby...we spend money.

There is an embroidery shop in Alabama that identified the "bonsai niche" and did something about it. They went to the National Arboretum in Washington, DC and licensed the rights to produce images of several of the trees in this world famous bonsai collection. These trees are the "holy grail" for bonsai fans, many even have names that they are known by and that are recognized by serious bonsai people. We also know the person who styled a particular specimen by name.

The embroidery shop offers a line of shirts, aprons, and hats that can be personalized with the image of one of these trees. The clothing comes in a variety of colors, and of course all sizes. They are "premium" priced for the bonsai market. Since they are made "to order" the store is not required to carry any additional inventory. By effectively using the internet and attending the major bonsai exhibits across the country, this enterprising entrepreneur has an ongoing "conversation" with his niche market.

How many embroidery shops are there across the country? I would bet a couple of thousand. Here is a great example of taking a commodity product, embroidered shirts, identifying a unique niche and servicing it. I tip my bonsai cap to this company!

2. A marketable product or service.

You can create all kinds of wonderful and wonky products and/or services but if no one wants what you've produced, what's the point? If you remember, I shared elsewhere about my friend who travelled to China with me and got the idea of marketing chicken feet here in the US. The niche market of people who enjoy eating fried chicken feet in this country is so small they probably wouldn't even fill a school bus.

There has to be enough of a demand for your product or service for your business to make a profit. How do you find out? By conducting market research...asking potential customers if they'd buy what you're thinking of selling. Fortunately, the internet has made this fast and cost efficient.

3. Choose a niche market that's available.

Remember, niche markets tend to be smaller so there's only room for so many players. When it comes to niche marketing, if you try to jump on a bandwagon, you're only going to fall off the back.

Before you started such a business yourself, you would certainly need to carefully research the competition and the size of the market to see if a new business in this niche would be viable.

4. Market, market, market.

Marketing is more important for niche market businesses than for any other kind, because the niche market business is by definition, unknown and succeeds or fails on making the connection with exactly the right kind of customer/client. If I open a Coffee Bean franchise, for example, people know right away what that business is about and what kinds of products to expect. And because Coffee Bean's market is "anybody who likes coffee", they really don't have to worry much about advertising at this point in the game.

If I open a business providing hand and finger physical therapy to the texting addict, handmade wild game sausages, or eco-tours to Belize, to give just three examples, people won't know what to expect or even that my niche business exists at all unless I make the effort to reach and educate them. Marketing becomes critical–and once you have a customer or client, make contact with them on a regular basis.

Those four steps can be helpful for someone looking to get into an opportunity.

What about a business owner who is looking to re-focus their business by identifying niche segments they can service profitably? Here are some questions for you:

- ✓ What is it that my current customers have in common?

- ✓ How do I separate myself from my competitors?

- ✓ What is unique about the service/product that I offer?

✓ What are the "extras" that I bring to the market?

Don't over think this. If you've had your business for awhile you know these answers already, maybe just haven't thought of them in this context. Write down the first couple of things that come to mind. Then, as you analyze this list, you should be able to identify one or more niche markets to go for.

The internet offers a powerful way to focus on an entire world of niches. People who enjoy herb gardening, raise ferrets, or cook Asian food are all examples of a type of niche. If you are in a brick and mortar business, or considering acquiring one, can you grow your business by marketing to aficionados of your niche worldwide? It would be easy to do. Why not:

✓ Identify blogs and forums that are related to your market. Join them.

✓ Optimize your website for the niche(s) you've targeted

✓ Create additional websites and/or squeeze pages to narrow the niche focus even more

✓ Establish yourself as a leader, a reliable "guru" within this niche by writing articles or even a book

Now consider the product or service you are thinking of

building a business around. Does it lend itself to being specifically tailored to a variety of niches? If yes, then spend some time thinking about how you can narrow the customer focus so that you can develop a marketing funnel for each of them. The more specifically you can target your audience, the higher return you will have on your marketing investment.

What Is My Opinion?

I said in an earlier chapter that "if everyone is your customer, then no one is your customer." I wasn't trying to be cute and coin a phrase. In fact, I can't even take credit for the phrase, I believe Dan Kennedy first used it.

Regardless of the source, it's true. Particularly for the small business owner. If you have a limited marketing budget, the more clearly you can identify very specific segments of your market place and design campaigns to appeal to them the more effective your advertising dollars will be.

Don't make the mistake of trying to be all things to all people. Identify the niches and watch your sales soar!

Gordon Van Wechel

Chapter 10

"Something is wrong. We don't know
what it is or where it is. Your job
will be to find it and fix it
before the end of the day."

Question #9: What Is The Company History? Who Are You Getting Into Bed With?

I'm going to guess that you didn't propose to your spouse after the first date. Of course not! You spent some period of months getting to know them as a person. In many cases, you met their family and friends as the relationship progressed. Finally, there came the day when you felt so comfortable with this person that you didn't want to consider the possibility that they would not be in your life.

It is amazing to me the number of people who attend a franchise seminar or group introductory meeting for a business opportunity, and then immediately jump aboard without performing any due diligence. The most basic questions often don't get asked at all.

What are those questions? More important, how do I find the answers? That's the subject of this chapter— what are some ways to properly investigate a company you are thinking about making an investment with. I'm going to suggest three techniques to do this. First, some questions to ask yourself as you review the company offering, franchise prospectus, or business brokers proposal. Second, a list of resources you can utilize to get "behind the brochure" and really learn more about the company. Third, a strategy to learn more about a company by examining its products.

Let's begin with the questions:

1. Is it clear <u>exactly</u> what you'll be doing?

Too often the prospectus from the company, or the sales information from the business broker is long on hyperbole and short on details. If you join this opportunity or purchase this business do you know precisely what you'll be selling? Is it clear what you will be doing each day as the owner?

This might seem to be too obvious, but in my experience there are endless opportunities touted online and in brochures as being the cream of the crop, the best of the best, the ultimate money-making opportunity destined to give you the freedom and flexibility you desire.

They just don't tell you HOW. I think that's important, don't you?

2. Can you independently find someone doing this business who is successful?

Every company has their superstar franchisees or distributors that are profiled in the magazine and business prospectus. What about just regular people doing the business? Can you find and talk with them?

A great place to look is on-line message boards and forums. If you are a Linked In member, look for industry groups or even specific company groups that you can join. These can be a fabulous source of first-hand information from people who have been there, done that. Ask for other people's experiences with an opportunity before you join. If you can find a number of people who have had good experiences, that's great. If you can't, and all you hear are negative comments, then learn from them. As I've said before, pioneers get scalped; settlers make money. Don't get scalped!

3. How long as the opportunity been around?

I'd like a track record of success before I put my time or money into an opportunity. Without this it's just too hard to predict how an average person coming into the industry can or will do. "Getting in on the ground floor" is not an incentive for me. It's far better to have a solid history that shows viability.

4. Are you selling an opportunity or a product?

Direct selling and network marketing companies often focus on earning income by signing up others and don't focus too much attention on their product(s). Technically, this is a violation of FTC requirements.

Every opportunity should allow you to earn an income by selling a product or service to customers. If it focuses primarily on recruiting, walk away.

5. Are the companies claims and testimonials verifiable?

Is contact information provided so that you can verify a testimonial? Can you find people who actually earn what the opportunity claims you can earn? Did they do it by following the suggested system provided by the company?

Income claims shouldn't be taken too seriously, especially if they're specific and a high number. Everyone's different. While one person may really do well with the business, that doesn't necessarily guarantee any success for you. A statement of actual average earnings is more useful. Franchise and network marketing companies are required to disclose actual income ranges and numbers of people achieving ranks within the company. Study this information carefully.

Exercise caution if an opportunity "guarantees" that you can make money. That is completely beyond their control; it's your efforts, your skills, and your motivation that determine whether or not you'll make money.

6. How does the company respond to your questions?

One thing I encourage you to do is ask a lot of questions by email or phone (they DO have contact information posted, right?). Do this over several conversations and try to speak with different people each time. If your questions are answered quickly, courteously, and with adequate detail; that's a good thing. Emails that are ignored or phone calls not returned are a bad sign. If they treat prospective affiliates that way, how do they treat their customers?

Can you physically visit the company headquarters, regional office, or manufacturing area? Is that something that is encouraged when you ask? If you are thinking about making a sizable investment in a franchise, or committing your time to a network marketing company, I'd encourage you to make every effort to personally visit the company.

7. Does the opportunity fit your interests?

Most of us have had jobs we hated, there is certainly no point to getting into a business we're not going to enjoy either. Is the product or service something you like and/or believe in? Does it require an attention to detail that you are comfortable with? If your idea of a perfect day at work is staring at your computer, are you going to be comfortable talking face to face with customers all day? You get the idea.

Learning About the Company From 3rd Party Sources

The Internet is a wonderful thing when it comes to research. Almost anything can be learned about a company and the people running it with just a little investment of time and keystrokes. Following are some sites that will help you. Some of these are membership sites, other require a fee to use. Most are free.

www.corporateinformation.com Current financial data on publicly traded companies.

www.asaecenter.org a comprehensive directory of business and professional associations

www.hoovers.com timely information on 50,000 public and private companies

www.business.com news, research, and contacts for more than 50,000 public and private companies

www.searchsystems.net a place to look for private company information

www.infospace.com helps locate a business, person, email address, and more. Has a "reverse look up" function that can be quite helpful.

www.superpages.com a database of over 16 million business listings

The company home page. Duh! Use Google to search for the company you are interested in and read their site.

www.sec.gov/edgar.shtml all public companies are required to file regular reports with the SEC. The "Edgar" database is where you can access them.

www.yahoo.com/finance contains detailed information on about 10,000 public companies www.dogpile.com searches the web for articles about the company you're researching

www.bizjournals.com gives access to all the articles in the 41 weekly business journals published across the country

Google Usenet allows you to search for discussions about companies and their products.

www.fuld.com This is a company that compiles detailed information on 27 different industry groups including many links to other sites.

www.findarticles.com is an extensive reference of business articles from more than 300 publications, both US and international

www.magportal.com similar to Find Articles

www.ipl.org a listing of over 2000 professional, academic, trade, and research organization

www.tsnn.com offers a continually updated listing of over 50,000 trade shows, conferences, and seminars during the year

www.thomasnet.com search regionally for information on more than a half million industrial and manufacturing companies

www.guidestar.org is a searchable directory of not for profit organizations

Don't forget the local Better Business Bureau and Chambers of Commerce.

Learning About the Company Through its Products

Another way to learn more about a company is to carefully examine and test its products. This can help you identify competitive market advantages or disadvantages of the product you are considering selling. The more completely you understand the benefits to your customer of the product or service you will be marketing, the better you can position your marketing spend to grow your business quickly.

Most of these criteria apply to product evaluation, many can also be used to review a service. They are also effective to use as you analyze the products your competitors offer. I realize that this list is probably more than most small business owners will ever need. That's OK, I want to impress on you the importance of doing this level of research. If for no other purpose than to be knowledgeable in the future when your customers ask you a question!

The product itself:

- ✓ What is it called and what is it intended to do?
- ✓ Is the product to be sold to business or consumer customers?

✓ Can the product be used by itself, or does it work in sync with something else? (for example: a bike light requires a bike.)
✓ Is it available in different sizes or colors? How many?
✓ Are there accessories that can be sold?
✓ Is the product available in various versions for different age groups?
✓ Is it consumable? Over what time period?
✓ Are there versions for different countries?
✓ How frequently are their model updates or new releases?
✓ Can it be customized with logos, mascots, colors?

Product competition:

✓ Is this a unique product...or a "me too?"
✓ Is the product readily available? At the store? On line?
✓ Are there relevant patents, copyrights, trademarks, URL's?
✓ How easily can the product be taken to another manufacturer?
✓ Is it being discounted on line through Ebay or other sites?

Ease of use:

✓ Does the product come assembled?
✓ Are there batteries required?
✓ Any unusual fuel, ink, electrical or other requirements?

✓ Are the ergonomics good?

✓ Is the design appealing?

✓ Is it a product that is easy to use right out of the box? Or does it require an instruction manual and/or documentation?

✓ Is that documentation easy to read and utilize? Written in multiple languages?

✓ Are there parts that will require replacement? Can this be done by the customer, or will it require a service tech person?

Marketing:

✓ Find an advertisement for the product. What features are being promoted?

✓ Does advertising appear to be a major expense in relation to the product cost?

✓ Where is the product being advertised? (newspaper, niche magazine, etc.)

✓ Is someone else advertising the product in your market area at this time?

✓ Is the product designed for specific niche(s), or can anyone be a potential customer?

That is a quick introduction to product analysis as a means of learning more about the company you're considering partnering with. You could take this to an extreme, but for most small business owners or franchisees that isn't necessary. What is important is to get a sense for the commitment to product quality and innovation that any company you choose to work with has.

What Is My Opinion?

I had an interesting conversation with a friend a couple of weeks before writing this. She had recently joined a popular network marketing company and kept inviting me to come to a "tasting." I knew she was inviting me to an opportunity meeting...but "tasting" sounds so much more civilized, don't you think?

I have a lot of respect for this person, so told her I'd think about trying to fit it in and to follow up with me the next week. I spent less than 30 minutes using many of the sites and reference procedures I've suggested to you. In that time I learned very specific information about the company, it's publically traded parent company, and the management team (most of whom had joined the company within the past six months). I learned that they had decided to grow their brand by offering successful distributors from other companies a bonus to cross over and represent this new company. I also was able to get very specific data on the formulation and nutrition science behind their product.

I was not a prospect for the business anyway, and based on what I learned from just a few minutes of due diligence I was even less interested. When I shared the reasons why with my friend most of what I had learned was new information to her.

This is not unusual. I'm often asked to consult with a business owner or network marketing distributor who is facing challenges in their business and soon realize they had not done any significant investigation before making a commitment. In one case my clients network marketing company had suddenly closed their doors and left him without the product he had already paid for or the commission earnings he had coming. In less than 10 minutes of research I learned that the two main principles of the company had presided over the start up and failure of two previous companies, filed personal bankruptcy, and reincorporated in another state.

What's the message? Do Your Homework!

I'm going to share information on the network marketing business model later in this book, but I want to give you a few quick analysis questions that anyone considering a company using this marketing method should ask. The fact is that more than 90% of these companies fail within the first five years, so it is important to choose wisely.

A key indication for companies this type of company is the number of distributors, and the retention rate of distributors from year to year. Ideally you are looking for a company with less than 200,000 active people. If they are losing 40% or more of their distributor base each year that is a bad sign.

The Federal Trade Commission is the regulatory agency that supervises all network marketing companies. They mandate that a company provide statistics on how many of their distributors actually achieve the various levels or ranks in their company. Find this data. If the company publishes an annual report these numbers could be included. You may find it buried on their website. If you don't, ask the customer service department for the data.

Don't be surprised to learn that a small fraction of the total distributor base actually reaches the upper third of the compensation scale in a network marketing company. It is quite common that something less than 1/2 of 1% of distributors make it to the top. In fact, often you'll see that less than 5% reach the top three or four levels, depending on how many ranks are in the company system.

Remember that in this business model your success is completely dependent on your own skills and work habits. If you are confident you can be successful, these statistics should not dissuade you from starting.

Any company attempting to sell you a franchise (also regulated by the FTC), is required to provide similar statistical data on the number of franchisees who are still active in their business based on years in the company. As you know, if you've read this far, there are many variables that determine the success of any business. However, if a high number of people who invest in a franchise concept quit three to five years later, that would make me question the viability of the company.

The bottom line is don't let you enthusiasm to begin a business get in the way of your good sense! Ask a lot of questions. If you're not getting the answers you want then move on to the next opportunity. It is a fact that there are plenty of good prospective businesses that are worthy of your time and money. Don't be in such a hurry that you don't get all the answers before investing.

Gordon Van Wechel

Chapter 11

*"Just remember, as CEO, you're a
role model for everyone -- just like
a sports hero or movie star....
after rehab, of course."*

Question #10: Is There An Opportunity To Get Wealthy With Leverage or Residual Income?

For me, this is the most important question of all the ten we have been discussing. All too often someone goes into business and has really just bought themselves a job. Usually it is a job that requires far more hours, higher risk, and lower earnings than the position they

Gordon Van Wechel

had previously. I understand that there is a sense of accomplishment that comes from creating and building a successful enterprise. It is also nice to know that you can walk away, for a time, or forever, from that enterprise and still enjoy a significant income stream.

Leverage is the ability to implement systems for control in your business and to identify and empower key individuals on your team. Why is this important? First, to free your time for the two critical activities that can only be done by you as the owner: marketing and innovating the business.
Second, so that you can, if you choose to, turn over day to day management of the enterprise to these key people. This allows you to create a new enterprise, or reduce your work schedule.

Residual income is money that you continue to earn after you have stopped running the business yourself. Please don't confuse residual income with a "passive" income that you can have after turning over your business to a group of employees or a management team. Residual income is true, "walk away" money that comes in each month without your effort or the effort of employees, maintaining inventory, or having to continue to put time into business growth.

There are only two business models that I am aware of

that can offer true residual income. The first is network marketing. Also referred to as "multi-level marketing," this business model is shunned by many who have had a negative experience themselves, or with a family member who has joined a network marketing company.

The second is Affiliate Marketing. With the growth of the internet and introduction of Web 2.0 capacity, a new twist on an old income stream was created, referred to as "Affiliate Marketing." This is the term used to describe promoting other people's products through affiliate links on a website. It is really no more than the owner of a product agreeing to pay you a commission or referral fee if you sell for them.

In Part Two of this book I'm going to offer a more thorough analysis of both the network marketing and affiliate marketing business models. If you are looking to find a business you can start with a minimal outlay of money, both of these models merit your consideration.

Both of these business models also lend themselves to a part time or second income. They provide a great opportunity for someone who is considering leaving their full time position to "try out" owning a business of their own before making a total commitment.

What Is My Opinion?

As I said in the first line of this chapter, the availability of an ongoing residual income is the most important consideration for me as I evaluate business opportunities. Admittedly that is a feeling based in large part on my age and the fact that I'm interested in slowing down a little. It also comes from reflecting back over a career that has had some significant successes and a couple of flaming failures as well. Having a steady, residual income can certainly be a leveling factor to balance out those extremes.

I believe strongly in the network marketing business model. I would recommend it to anyone who is looking to create a secondary income to supplement their job or career earnings. I have also encouraged men and women who are investigating beginning a second career to consider looking for a network marketing company with products or services they are comfortable working with. If I were given the choice of investing my life savings and borrowing even more to buy a business that would become my new job, or investing less than $1000 in a carefully selected network marketing company and working that business; I'd choose the network marketing company 100% of the time!

I am almost as bullish on affiliate marketing. With almost no investment it is possible to create an ongoing stream of income from multiple sources. The challenges in this business model are that it does require a little more technical computer knowledge than many people have. The ultimate goal of any web based marketing program is to create a large, responsive list of prospects. This can be done through multiple channels, but again requires a higher level of sophistication with the computer.

Both network and affiliate marketing take time and consistent effort to build a successful business. Both can be "scaled" to a substantial income. I know people in both models who are earning high five and even six figure incomes monthly.

This is a good example of the relativity of time. I tell people who are considering either of these businesses that it will take them two to five years to build an income of $25,000 a month or more. That is two to five years of diligent work following a plan. Stop and think about that for a minute. If you continue to work hard at your current career, what are the chances that your company is going to pay you $25,000 a month five years from now? Yeah, I thought so. That is the appeal of network and affiliate marketing. They are perhaps the last bastion of true free enterprise our economy offers.

Gordon Van Wechel

Part Two:

Applying The Ten Vital Questions In The "Real World"

Gordon Van Wechel

Chapter 12

LITTLE HINGES SWING BIG DOORS: THE BASIC EQUATION OF BUSINESS

In chapter one I wrote about the alarming number of businesses that fail in their first couple of years. Not having clear goals and a plan to achieve them I suggested was the primary cause. Now I want to propose a third reason, which is not understanding the Basic Equation of business.

The "Basic Equation" is the name I use to describe the complete flow of a business from the very beginning, finding a lead; right through to the end: you as the owner putting profits into your pocket. I first heard this concept in a presentation by Australian businessman Brad Sugars. He was speaking at a conference I attended in Las Vegas and talked about the "business chassis." The following day I was fortunate to be seated at his table for a luncheon, and he elaborated on the idea. I don't know or understand cars, so I've changed the metaphor a bit, but the essence of the equation is the same.

In this chapter I'm going to first share with you the components of the equation, then give you some examples of how it works in a real business with real numbers. I firmly believe, and this has been proven with my own clients, that once you understand the Basic Equation of Business you will never look at your own enterprise the same way again.

I think it was Dan Kennedy who said that, "little hinges swing big doors." That is really the concept I want to share with you in this chapter. Once you understand the Basic Equation you will have the power to effect big swings for your company.

Let me first list the components of the equation and their relationship, then I'll elaborate on each one of them. For those of you who labor under the mistaken notion that "my business is different" and assume this doesn't apply to you...well, you're wrong! Whether you manufacture widgets or sell ice cream or help people out of their legal problems--this equation applies to your business. So open your mind and see how understanding can lead to more profits. After all, isn't that why you have a business?

The Basic Equation has eight components. I'll list them, as well as put the "operator" in between each component so you can see how they work together.

1. Leads (prospects or potential customers)

Multiplied by

2. Conversion Rate (the difference between those that could have bought and those that did)

Equals

3. Customers (the total number of different customers you deal with)

Multiplied by

4. Number of Transactions (the average number of times each customer buys in a year)

Multiplied by

5. Average Dollar Sale Price (the average price of the items you sell)

Equals

6. Sales (the total amount of business done in a given time period)

Multiplied by

7. Margins (the percentage of each sale that is profit)

Equals

8. Profit (the reason you own your business and work so hard)

Now that you've seen the Equation, let's further define each component.

Your Number of Leads--the total number of potential buyers that you contacted or that contacted you in the last year (or whatever increment of time you want to measure). Most business people confuse responses, the number of potential buyers, with results. Just because the phone is ringing doesn't mean the cash register is.

What is even more surprising is the reality that very few businesses have an idea how many leads they actually get in a week, let alone have a method for determining the specific marketing campaign that they came from. It's a good thing to get a lot of leads, but then you've got to remember your...

Conversion Rate--The percentage of people who did buy as opposed to those who inquired. For example, if you had ten people walk into your store today but only four purchased anything, then you have a conversion rate of 4 out of 10, or 40%. This is, for most businesses, the fastest and easiest way to increase profits. You already have someone interested in your product or service, now you just have to get them to take the last step and buy.

When I have this conversation with most business owners, they have no idea what their conversion rate really is. Typically they will guess high--like 60%. Then when we actually put some metrics in place and measure, the result is more like 20%. This might seem disappointing, but it's really a blessing in disguise. Imagine how your business will run when the conversion rate is increased to 40%, or even higher. If you double your conversion rate you double your profit!

Number of Customers--This is the total number of different customers you deal with in a period of time. It is the product of the number of leads times your conversion rate. Most business owners who do not understand the Basic Equation can be heard saying, "oh, if I only had more customers." That says they haven't yet realized how business works. The number of customers is a result, not a variable. To increase you customer count you need more leads and/or a higher conversion rate.

Number of Transactions--This is another of the five variables in the equation. Some customers will buy from you frequently, other just occasionally, and still others just once in a lifetime. The number you are trying to determine here is the average number of times a customer buys from you in a year. Don't consider just the best customers, or the worst--it's the average that is important.

This is another place in the equation where an incremental change can have a huge impact on profits. In today's business environment it is a simple exercise to collect a database of customers. Most owners do not take the time to do this. Big Mistake! A simple postcard, phone call, even an email inviting them to come back will yield big profits.

Average Dollar Sale--This is a number that most business owners are familiar with. It's a simple calculation: take your total sales and divide by the number of sales made.

Sales--This is another multiplication problem. Multiply the total number of customers by the average number of times they shop with you, and then by the average amount they spend. That result is your sales, sometimes called "turnover." Most owners will have an idea about turnover, often relating it to how many times a year they "turn over" their inventory. That's thinking in the right direction, but doesn't fully grasp the idea of this number, how it is calculated, or most important, how to impact this figure.

Margins--The percentage of each and every sale that is profit. This is likely going to be different for each product or service you sell, but the calculation is easy. If you sell something for $100 and after all the costs of your business are taken out you have $10 left over, then you have a 10% margin.

Profit--Of course another result that we all want more of. Once again, you cannot directly get more profit. What you can do is increase your margin on the sales you have.

So there you have it--the Basic Equation of Business in all its glorious simplicity. This equation is the model that determines the profit level of every business on earth.

Once you realize that by analyzing your business using this equation, and focusing your attention on the five variables that you can control, you are ahead of the vast majority of business owners in the marketplace.

To prove beyond a reasonable doubt the power of this formula let's put some numbers into the equation, and then do some simple "what if" scenarios. Here we go:

1. Leads: 1000

Multiplied by

2. Conversion Rate: 25%

Equals

3. Customers: 250

Multiplied by

4. Number of Transactions: 2

Multiplied by

5. Average Dollar Sale Price: $100

Equals

6. Sales: $50,000

Multiplied by

7. Margin: 25%

Equals

8. Profit: $12,500

Now let's have some fun. What happens when you can increase each of the variables by just 10%? Logic says your profit should increase by 10% too, right? Get your calculator and check my math:

1. **Leads: 1100**

Multiplied by

2. **Conversion Rate: 27.5%**

Equals

3. **Customers: 302**

Multiplied by

4. **Number of Transactions: 2.2**

Multiplied by

5. **Average Dollar Sale Price: $110**

Equals

6. **Sales: $73,084**

Multiplied by

7. **Margin: 27.5%**

Equals

8. **Profit: $20,098**

WOW! Profit didn't increase by 10%, more like over 60%! Just by adding a 10% improvement in each of the variables you increase your profits by over 60%.

Shall we do one more? Let's assume that, over a period of time and with diligent work, you could double each of the variables. Again, logic would dictate that your profits would double...but I don't think I can fool with that one again. So let's check and see how the numbers work out (grab your calculator!)

Here's what happens when you DOUBLE the variables:

1. Leads: 2000

Multiplied by

2. Conversion Rate: 50%

Equals

3. Customers: 1000

Multiplied by

4. Number of Transactions: 4

Multiplied by

5. Average Dollar Sale Price: $200

Equals

6. Sales: $80,000

Multiplied by

7. Margin: 50%

Equals

8. Profit: $40,000

Your immediate reaction might be, "that's a silly example. It is unrealistic to think you can double each of the variables." But is it? The Japanese have a word, 'Kaizen'. It's a word they use to describe the effort to always be improving your results. In fact, the literal translation is "constant improvement."

Apply Kaizen to your business. What if you were able to improve each of the variables by just 1% a week, or even just 1% a month. Where would you be in a year? In five years? You've already committed your time and energy to the business, what about focusing on incremental changes in each of these areas?

Of course that sounds good, but how to do it is the million dollar question. I have written about how to do that elsewhere. You can check out my Total Market Takeover books written for specific business niches (but the concepts are applicable to any business) or my short book on how to implement just one strategy, the Capture Your Neighborhood Formula. (How's that for a shameless plug?)

Remember, little hinges swing big doors!

Chapter 13

" I won't be in tomorrow - I've caught
a computer virus."

Advanced Market Analysis

I mentioned in an earlier chapter that I wanted to expose you to some of the tools that well managed companies utilize to study the market positions of their products. How do the "big boys" know when to release a new product, and just how to position it within their product niche? Ever wonder why a company takes a product that you've been buying for years and suddenly re-packages, re-formulates, and re-releases it? Did you ever put the remote control down and actually watch a television commercial and then wonder who that advertisement had been designed for? Or why the company presented their product that way?

One answer is to all of these questions is advanced market analysis. Companies pay millions each year on focus groups, surveys, armies of MBA's with charts and graphs...all in an effort to better understand what you and I "really want" and to target their marketing spend to hitting that spot.

As small business owners we can't compete at that level. We can, and must, invest the time necessary to thoroughly understand the market place that we operate in, and the competitive challenges within our niche. The purpose of this chapter is to dig a little deeper into some of the analysis tools that will help you make wise decisions about how to invest your marketing time and money.

By doing this is a separate chapter I'm trying to strike and effective compromise. I believe that this information is important to understand, even at the basic level I'm going to be able to share here. Yet, I recognize that many of my readers are in a home based business where this type of analysis is not critical to your success. Others operate a franchise where the parent company has done a great deal of this work for you. Some of you however, will grow your companies to the place where you'll want to begin to broaden your marketing reach, and this knowledge will be valuable. Others may consider hiring a consultant or business growth specialist and will need to understand their vocabulary and methods.

There are numerous tools that you can use in analyzing both your business and potential business opportunities. I'm only going to share three. The first, identifying your customer avatar, is non-negotiable for anyone who owns or wants to own a business. It is one of the first exercises I do with clients looking to grow their business. The other two, SWOT and STEEPLE analysis are a little more esoteric. Valuable to work on, but not, in my opinion, as critical to your business growth and success. As your business matures and you are able to step back and think more about working "on" your business and not just "in" it, these two tools will have greater significance.

With that as background, let's jump into some of the tools used in advanced market analysis.

1. Creating your Prospect/Customer Avatar

One of the characteristics of successful companies is that they have a very clear idea of who their ideal customer is. They have invested time and resources in an effort to be absolutely certain they know as much as possible about the person who buys their products or services. More than just know them, they continue to invest in understanding how their ideal customer evolves over time.

We often call this person your "customer avatar." When we use that term we're identifying a representative customer or a personification of many people that comprise your target market. If you have not done this type of exercise it can be quite revealing.

I want to take you through a system that we use with our consulting clients. This is another one of those times when you'll want to have your pad and pen handy and spend some time thinking about your current customers if you are already in business, or project who you think will be ideal prospects for the business you contemplate creating. First, a clear definition of the scope of the project.

What is a prospect avatar?

- ✓ A specific person that you have identified as someone who is a likely user of your product or service, or who already uses it
- ✓ Not "a named person" but a representative of your target person, an "idealization"

✓ You can, and should, have more than one avatar, but each is unique—do not mix them up based on a single criteria. It is important to identify and recognize several avatars. That means you have multiple potential customers, and you will market to them in unique ways.

✓ If yours is a specialty business, then it is likely that you have things in common with your avatar

✓ You understand this person, through direct experience or significant study

✓ Your avatar is likely someone you would enjoy knowing or even working closely with

Now, work through the following questions to hone in on the specific characteristics of your avatar(s). The goal is to thoroughly consider their demographic, geographic, and psychographic data.

1. Who is your prospect? Pretend your prospect is sitting across from you right now... define him or her in great detail. How old are they? What gender? Where do they live? Are they married? Have kids? How much education do they have? What is their individual or family income range?

2. What does your avatar REALLY want? What are their inner core desires? What do they like and dislike? What are their interests or passions?

3. What are their major HOT points? What is it that they want to accomplish by using your product or service?

4. What are their top fears and frustrations- what keeps them up at night? What makes them mad? What do they worry about?

5. What are their top wants and desires? What's the outcome that they really want in whatever area of their lives that we can have input in? What are they really after? What is the end goal they think they want?

6. What does your product do or give your prospect that he or she doesn't know about? What is going to be most appealing about your product/service to your prospect?

I teach a marketing class for new business owners through the Service Corps of Retired Executives (SCORE). One of the concepts I stress to the participants is to focus on understanding their prospective customers more than just talking about their product or service.

To help them better grasp this concept I use the phrase, "If you want to know what John Smith buys, you have to see the world through John Smith's eyes." In this case

"John Smith" is one of their avatars; and the point of the exercise is to try and understand a customer's needs and motivations rather than just focus on what you sell.

I also teach them what we call "discovery questions." Here again the purpose of the exercise is to help the business owner better understand their prospective customer. Here are the questions:

1. Under what circumstances does the typical prospect start to think about buying what you sell?

What we're trying to understand is the prospects need for your product/service. What events might be going on in their lives to prompt their thinking about purchasing what you offer?

2. What things are important to your prospect when buying what you sell? Consider both the product or service itself, AND the buying process. Think about what prospects want AND what they want to avoid.

Very few business owners pay attention to what the customer experiences during the buying process. Not just the process of working with your business, but the general perception of your industry.

An example I use to illustrate this with my SCORE students is my distaste for the process of buying a car. From walking onto a dealers lot, being confronted by a salesperson, trying to understand all the "car speak" they use, negotiating a deal, then all the "up-sells" for products I've never heard of...I hate buying a vehicle!

Think about each facet of the customer experience in your industry. With your company. What can you do to help the prospect feel more comfortable with the process? How can you incorporate that emphasis on customer experience into your marketing?

3. What are the relevant and important issues that a prospect needs to be aware of when making a decision about what you sell?

Answering the questions that a prospect asks when shopping for your product or service is easy. All of your competitors do that. What about the questions a prospect doesn't know to ask? What about the details and potential problems that can only be understood through experience with your product or service?

If you take the time to identify these, and then bring them up to the prospect during the buying process, you will enhance your credibility and their trust in you and your company.

4. What do YOU do to give the customer what he or she wants?

As you continue to develop and refine your customer avatars, you'll be better positioned to respond directly to the real priorities that are in the mind of a prospect considering buying what you offer.

I heard a humorous quip from a speaker recently. He said, "in the land of the blind, the one-eyed man is king." I share that because in almost every business category I've ever consulted the typical owner is so focused on their own perception of what a customer is looking for that they never stop to actually listen to the prospect.

If you can avoid falling victim to that way of thinking, if you can stay focused on understanding the real desires of your prospect, and effectively communicate this attitude to prospects; you will be that "one-eyed man."

Many times when we begin this exercise, it is the first time our client has actually stopped and thought about what might be important to their customer. It can be a very revealing experience! Most of us as business owners are so focused on what we offer that we rarely stop and think about how a prospective client views or experiences our company and our team. It can be sobering to realize how much money we have left on the table over the time we've been in business because of this ignorance.

I hope you have taken this exercise seriously. Understanding your customer in a deep, almost an intimate way, can save you thousands of dollars in wasted marketing. As you get to know your avatar you will intuitively make new product and business growth decisions with them in mind. Your business will grow as a result.

2. S.W.O.T. Analysis. This is a strategic planning method developed in the 1970's as a tool for deciding whether to proceed with a specific project or business growth strategy. It was popular with Fortune 500 companies and quickly became a staple part of business school curriculum. That doesn't mean that it isn't valuable to the entrepreneur starting out or the small business owner. You should incorporate this methodology into your market analysis.

S.W.O.T stands for: strengths, weaknesses, opportunities, and threats. The purpose in completing the analysis is to identify key internal and external factors that could be important to the decision you are trying to make. That decision could be to as simple as introducing a new product line to whether to open a satellite location in a new city. SWOT analysis groups key pieces of information into two main categories:

- ✓ Internal factors –
  The *strengths* and *weaknesses* internal to your business
- ✓ External factors –
  The *opportunities* and *threats* presented by outside factors

To give you a little better idea of how SWOT works, I'll give you a typical series of questions that you might use when implementing this tool. These are not the "right" or "only" questions, just an example to stimulate your thinking.

Strengths:

- ✓ What are the advantages I have in my business?
- ✓ What are the core competencies of our staff?
- ✓ Where are we making the most money?
- ✓ What do we do really well?
- ✓ Do we have superior staff or products?
- ✓ Great location?

Weaknesses:

- ✓ Where do we lack resources?
- ✓ What do we do badly?
- ✓ Where are we losing money?
- ✓ Are there aspects of our business that we are avoiding?
- ✓ What needs to be improved?
- ✓ Is our cost structure too high?
- ✓ Is our reputation with customers poor?

Opportunities:

- ✓ Are there beneficial trends that we are taking advantage of?
- ✓ New technologies?

- ✓ Niches our competitors are not in?
- ✓ New customer needs we can meet?
- ✓ Loosening of government regulations (ok, that's a joke!)

Threats:

- ✓ Aggressive competitors?
- ✓ Negative economic conditions?
- ✓ Government regulation?
- ✓ Changing business climate?
- ✓ Successful competitors?
- ✓ Increasing trade barriers
- ✓ Technology changes that affect our current product?

One way of utilizing SWOT is matching and converting. Matching is used to find competitive advantages by matching the strengths to opportunities. Converting is applying strategies to convert weaknesses or threats into strengths or opportunities. For example, finding new markets. If the threats or weaknesses cannot be converted, another plan to minimize or avoid them must be developed.

3. STEEPLED Analysis. Don't you just love business school acronyms? This tool is a more recent innovation. Think of it as a 20,000 foot view of the challenges to your business. Said another way, if SWOT analysis focuses on specific and direct challenges to your business; STEEPLED analysis asks you to consider the macro influences that can impact your business. Here are the definitions:

Social--factors include the cultural aspects affecting business, health consciousness, population growth rate, age distribution, career attitudes and emphasis on safety. These social trends can affect the demand for a company's products and how that company operates. For example, an aging population may imply a smaller and less-willing workforce (thus increasing the cost of labor).

Technological-- factors include influences such as R&D activity, automation, the rate of technological change, and government incentives used to implement new technologies. Technology changes can affect barriers to entry, revise production levels and influence outsourcing decisions. Technological shifts can affect costs, quality, and lead to innovation.

Economic-- factors include economic growth, interest rates, exchange rates and the inflation rate. Currency exchange rates affect the costs of exporting goods and the supply and price of imported goods.

Ethical—factors reflect changing social norms and how quickly they can impact a business. For example, you market a product that is made overseas in an area that is notorious for employing children in factories, and how that fact affects consumer buying decisions.

Political—factors are how and to what degree a government intervenes in the economy. Specifically, political factors include areas such as tax policy, labor law, environmental law, trade restrictions, tariffs, and political stability.

Legal--factors include discrimination law, consumer law, antitrust law, employment law, and health and safety law. These factors can affect how a company operates, its costs, and the demand for its products.

Environmental—a company's "environmental footprint" has become an important consideration for many consumers. Being a "good environmental citizen" is a distinct marketing advantage employed by innovative marketers.

Demographic—factors include a careful analysis of your customer avatar(s) and their changing behaviors. Where are they in life: single high consumers, young families building a nest, empty nesters with discretionary income?

7. Building Your Strategic Plans. Once you have completed your competitive analysis, you can proceed with the final step in the process: building a strategic marketing plan. I've written earlier about the importance of a business plan. Your strategic marketing plan is a part of this overall business plan. It is, in my opinion, the most important aspect of your business plan and should be reviewed and updated at least monthly as you grow your business.

What Is My Opinion?

A legitimate criticism of all these analysis tools is that can become easy to confuse activity with accomplishment. What I mean by this is you may spend a lot time compiling lists rather than thinking about what is actually important in achieving your objectives. These tools also present data uncritically and without clear prioritization. For example, weak opportunities may appear to balance strong threats if you're just looking at a chart and not focusing on a realistic interpretation of the data.

Here's what I tell my clients:

1. Know your customer avatar(s). Get so deeply inside your customers mind that when you're talking with a customer it feels like you are looking in the mirror and

hearing yourself ask the question. There is no amount of statistical analysis or research that will substitute for spending time with those you are marketing to. Only when you develop that know-like-trust relationship will your business really be on a solid foundation.

Here's a side benefit to focusing on your customer. As you continue the conversation with them, they will provide direction for your growth and increased prosperity. Want to add new products to your offerings? Your customers will tell you what they want. Isn't it a whole lot more efficient to bring into stock a new product where the market is already established? Want to head off a problem before it becomes critical? Your customers, if you are in regular dialogue with them, will tell you where you're slipping.

2. Keep track of your competition. Incorporate into your normal pattern of management regular times to study what is going on in your market place. Visit your competitor. Spend time on his/her website. Talk with their customer service people. Do they have a new product available? Are their business hours changing? Do you belong to trade associations? What innovations are happening in your industry that you can be first to the market with in your area? Never lose sight of the fact that someone out there wants your customer. Keep a close eye on the rear view mirror.

3. Be your best you. There is a reason you are in business, or thinking about getting into business. What is it? What skill set or advantage do you have that drives you to take the risk of having your own company? Don't get so involved in the outside influences on your business that you lose sight of the core strength that you bring to the marketplace. Don't let yourself get so buried working in your business that you forget to keep working on yourself.

4. Assume that things will change in your market. Right now, in a dorm room on a university campus, probably not in the US, a student is sitting in front of a computer inventing something that will affect your business. Maybe not tomorrow, but you can be 100% certain that innovation and transformation is coming. You will adjust, or fail.

5. It's OK to put your needs first. We live in an era where personal choice is greater than at any time in history. The computer and internet have made it possible for a stay at home mom to sit at her kitchen table and be successful creating an international business. A dad who wants to spend more time with his kids can step off the corporate treadmill and using his expertise and a little technology consult with clients across borders and time zones.

This is a great time to be alive! Don't get so bogged down cutting the weeds that grow in your business garden that twenty years from now you can't remember the flowers in the Spring. If your business isn't meeting your desires or the needs of your family—then change it. You don't have to settle any more. That's why I wrote this book, to prove to you that there are business opportunities that you can take advantage of that offer a lifestyle and not just a company.

Choose wisely!

Chapter 14

"It appears to be some sort of pyramid scheme."

Is Network Marketing the Right Business For You?

Several times in this book I mention the Network Marketing business model. For many, joining a Network Marketing company might be the perfect answer to creating a second source of income. The purpose of this chapter is to help you make that decision.

What Is Network Marketing? In this chapter I'll be

161

answering that question, as well as giving you valuable answers to several important questions related to this unique industry and business model. These include:

> ➢ How does a network marketing company work?
> ➢ What should I look for in a good network marketing company?
> ➢ How do I get started in network marketing?
> ➢ Why do so many people fail at network marketing?
> ➢ What are the key factors that will make YOU successful with this business model?

Before we jump into answering those questions, let me briefly share some of my personal experiences with the industry. The purpose of doing so is to help you learn from both the successes I have enjoyed and the failures I have endured while learning how network marketing works. It is these experiences that have proven to be valuable to my clients looking for a home based business and my team members in the company that I am affiliated with.

 Thirty years ago I received a telephone call from my Uncle Gus. I had recently moved to Denver, my Aunt and Uncle's home town. I had a great deal of respect for Gus. He had built and sold two large manufacturing companies in his career and retired before his 60th birthday. Gus called to say he was starting a new venture and wanted me to be involved in it with him. I jumped at the chance, and later that week went over to their home "to meet some of his associates." This was my first network marketing "in home opportunity meeting."

There was an experienced distributor who told his story and using a white board drew out the business model and how we'd make money. Honestly, I didn't understand too much at that point, but if Uncle Gus was going to do it, so was I! That very week I began telling my friends about this great new deal I was getting involved in. Of course I'd had zero training and was not able to answer any of their questions, but that didn't stop me.

Today I refer to that kind of enthusiasm as "ignorance on fire!"

Gus and I did that business for the next 12 months. Conducted regular opportunity meetings, went to national events, subscribed to the weekly training audiotape program—all the activities that were supposed to lead to success. We didn't make much money, and finally realized that all our work was producing almost no cash flow. Gus was my "sponsor," and his sponsor was at the other end of the country. We were orphans. We quit the business.

On the surface this first foray into network marketing was a failure. Looking back, that is not the case. Rather, it began a lifelong fascination with this business model and how people succeed at it. During the year that Gus and I tried to build an organization, I had several opportunities to meet and talk with successful distributors. Men, women, and couples who were earning $50,000 or more PER MONTH. That opened my eyes to the financial power in this business model.

More important, I learned the incredible power of "the dream." Most of the people who were in that company were like Gus and I, rookies trying to figure out what to do, and usually not too successful at it. But what had made us join the company, and kept us going during the inevitable struggles, was our dream...what each of us saw at the end of the network marketing rainbow.

"The Dream" is what motivates a person to come home from a long day at work, grab a quick dinner, then go out to a meeting where there is a decent chance that no prospects will show up. "The Dream" causes a family to pack the car, load up the kids, and drive for twelve hours to attend an event and affiliate with successful people. It's "The Dream" of financial freedom and what that means to each individual that propels them to keep trying. This is an incredibly powerful emotion that is at the foundation of everyone that I've met who is successful in a network marketing company.

Since that first experience, I've built and sold several traditional companies. I've also joined and worked in three other network marketing companies. Two because I really liked the products and wanted to buy them at wholesale, the other I worked to build a business with residual income.

I strongly believe in the networking business model. It can be a powerful road to financial and time independence. For that to happen, the combination of product, market timing, compensation plan, and company size all need to be in alignment. More important, you as the independent distributor for that company need to have the right mindset for success in this unique business model.

So let's look more closely at the model, answering the questions I posed earlier. The purpose of this analysis is to enable you to more accurately determine if a network marketing company is the right fit for you at this time in your life. I also want to give you some criteria to use in evaluating the numerous opportunities out there in the marketplace.

What Is Network Marketing?

At its most simple, network marketing is a method of distribution of products/services that utilizes independent representatives to reach potential customers that would otherwise be difficult to market to with traditional online or offline marketing strategies. To do this, network marketing distributors invite their friends, family, and associates to utilize the company products and share the business opportunity with their circle of influence.

It may surprise you to learn that many businesses that we think of as "traditional" utilize the exact same business model. Insurance, real estate, and mortgage salespeople are almost always "independent agents" of their companies. Their parent company many times will provide advertising and marketing material for the agents to use, but the agent is an independent contractor with the company, not an employee.

As a contrast, you will rarely see a company that uses the network marketing business model doing large scale advertising or promoting of their products. That is why they have a "network" of independent associates sharing with their contacts.

Another distinction is market territories. In the network marketing environment you are not restricted to a specific geographical area to market in. In fact, you are encouraged to market anywhere in the world where the company is licensed to conduct business. It is this "unlimited" potential that is one of the primary incentives to join a network marketing company.

Why Does A Company Choose The Network Marketing Business Model?

Think for a moment about the financial investment necessary to "roll out" a new product line, or introduce a new company to the marketplace. Full page ads in USA Today, radio and television, billboards in key markets...it can easily cost tens of millions of dollars to bring a new product to market. Most start-up companies don't have this kind of money to invest. They also recognize that the most powerful kind of marketing is "word of mouth." If they can help you get happily involved with their product or service, and provide a reasonable incentive for you to tell your family and friends about it, that "word of mouth" advertising will help them grow. Granted, it may be a slower growth curve than advertising on the NBC Nightly News, but it's also millions of dollars less expensive.

Thirty years ago the rule was that only "consumable" products lent themselves to the network marketing business model. That is, a product that you used over and over and needed to replenish each month. That is no longer the case. Today we see all kinds of products being marketed through "networks." These include communication services, legal assistance, solar power, weight loss, water treatment, financial planning, internet access, nutrition, skin care, just to name a few.

There is another, non-financial, reason that a company chooses the network marketing business model for their product or service. That is the huge number of people who are looking for an opportunity to better their financial circumstances. For a lot of people their day to day job or career is limiting, they know that they will never be able to advance to a level that will provide the lifestyle and comfort that they want ("The Dream") for themselves and their families. Part of the allure of a network marketing business is that it is designed to start on a part time basis. Most people work five to ten hours a week at the beginning, learning the business and developing their skills until they can effectively replace their "regular job" income with their "part time job" income. Network marketing companies encourage this pattern of growth, and a good company has training and incentive programs specifically designed to help the new part time associate get started and realize small successes early in their career.

Bottom line: if you want to call your own shots in life, if you're willing to get the education you will need to run a small business, if you enjoy working with people, then network marketing just might be the right kind of business for you. On the other hand, if you're only in it for the money or just don't like dealing with people, you will most likely fail.

With the economy the way it is today, working from home as an affiliate of a good network marketing company may make more sense than acquiring a second job in order to make ends meet. That is if you can find a decent second job!

How Does Network Marketing Work?

According to the Direct Selling Association there are approximately 17 million people in the US involved with some type of network marketing business. Would it surprise you to know that network marketing is a hugely successful business model in other countries as well? In fact, several of the largest network marketing companies in the world do not even market to the United States! So how does this business model actually work?

Each day millions of people report to their jobs, where their employer leverages there time to build his or her business. As employees, we trade hours for dollars.

In network marketing we assist others in building their business, and in doing so grow our own as well. We're teaching them how to leverage their time, with all of us gathering customers along the way. Thus the name "network." We get paid for this because we are assisting, coaching, and helping our associates establish and build their business.

If you were to build a traditional business, you would need the investment capital to acquire the business, plus financial reserves to support the ongoing enterprise until it is profitable. These costs can add up quite quickly, particularly when you factor in occupancy costs, tax and other government expenses, staff hiring and training, inventory, etc.

In network marketing our initial investment in business start up costs is anywhere from just a few dollars to several hundred dollars. This is certainly much lower than the cost of acquiring a traditional business. You will also have some ongoing expense for training and advertising, business tools, travel, etc. One reason that people do not succeed in a network marketing business is that they fail to consider the nominal ongoing costs to be in business.

Perhaps the most important thing to remember is that **you are in a real business!** It is your own business, you no longer have a boss holding you accountable. Your success or failure is totally dependent on YOU. Your new job is to gather customers for your product or service and to help others get started in their own business partnered with you. This is a business model that will take **3 to 5 years of working 5 to 20 hours a week** to produce the kind of success you're looking for. This is not a get rich quick overnight program.

A common question that I am asked with helping people decide on a business is "will I have to sell the product or service?" The short answer is yes. But this is a different kind of selling than you might initially think. In network marketing we share and recommend products that we like and personally use. Remember the last time you saw a movie you really enjoyed? How many people did you tell about the movie? Or a great experience at a new restaurant? Or who has a mechanic for their car that they trust and recommend to their friends?

That's what we do in Network Marketing. We share and recommend. Yes, it is selling...but not in the traditional sense.

Getting Started In Network Marketing

Truthfully, it is far too easy to start a networking marketing business! You get invited to a meeting, get excited about the product/service/income potential; fill out a couple of forms, make a small investment, and you're there. You have your own business! Now what?

If you're fortunate enough to have a good sponsor, they

will set aside some time to train you on both the product and how to grow the business. Many companies have standardized tools to support this effort as well. If your sponsor is new to the business, or long distance, your success might be more difficult.

Before jumping into the first company you are exposed to, let me suggest a due diligence process that includes five critically important areas.

1. Integrity. Does the company have it? Do they stand behind their products, services, and distributors? Do they make believable claims about the products/services? Is what you're hearing about the company, product, and profitability reasonable? This is a good time to remember the old adage, "If it sounds too good to be true, it probably is."

2. Distributor Driven. Does the company make decisions that protect both the company's long term success as well as the success of the individual distributor? Are there tools and marketing materials that will help you succeed? Do these tools evolve as the marketplace changes?

3. Products and Services. Do you like what you're considering selling? If you are not enthused about

the product or service you are recommending, it is going to be difficult to grow a business. Is the product/service something that is desired by a lot of people? Just because you love it doesn't mean there is a market out there. Is the product/service something that you can visualize your family/friends/associates wanting? If not, you are going to have a tough time getting started, since we all begin with people who already know, like, and trust us.

4. Is the business system easily duplicated? More important, can you visualize yourself working successfully within the business system offered by the company? What if your sponsor quits the week after you get started? Are there tools and training programs in place so that you can still succeed without them? There are really only two essential things that you will need to be successful: first, the willingness to learn; and second, the ability to take action.

5. Management. Good management is critically important in this business model. What is the experience of the people running the company? Do they have a business resume that demonstrates integrity? Where have they worked in the past? Do they have experience in network

marketing? These are easy questions to answer using Google.

Network marketing is a powerful and compelling business model. Don't let your enthusiasm get in the way of common sense when getting started!

Network Marketing Compensation Plans

How you get paid in network marketing is far from standardized. Plans vary from company to company, and it is not uncommon for a company to modify their plan occasionally as the company grows or market conditions change. Here are some general rules:

➢ If someone upline from you cannot help you understand the basics of how you get paid in ten minutes or less then you can be sure you, as a new person, are going to have a problem sharing this with people you show the opportunity to. Simple is better!

➢ If the total payout is greater than 60% of the product price you should be suspect. That typically means that the product is overpriced. There may be an exception, like an exclusive patent, but that is unusual.

➢ What is the monthly usage requirement to qualify for commissions? Most companies are going to require a certain amount of product usage each month by a distributor if they want to earn the maximum from their business. Is that amount reasonable for you to achieve each month?

➤ If you miss your monthly usage requirement, what happens to your business?

➤ Is the comp plan front end or back end pay? When do you get paid, and based on what?

➤ Many comp plans have names. You'll hear terms like binary, matrix, uni-level, stair step, and others. The difference generally has to do with how many people you have on your front line and how many levels of depth you get paid on.

In my experience, what the plan is called is less important than how quickly and easily you can explain the basics to a prospect so they understand what they need to do initially to achieve success! Let me say it again: Simple is better!

Why So Many People Fail in Network Marketing

If this is such an easy business model, why are there so many really smart and hard working people that fail to build a business that can support them? I've heard many reasons over the years.

1. Training. The company they affiliated with, or the sponsor they followed, didn't support them with a good training program.

2. The company "changed" or just went out of business.

3. "The person who sponsored me misrepresented the business."

4. "I couldn't put in as many hours as I found it really required."

5. "The compensation plan wasn't fair, newer people couldn't get ahead."

I could go on listing reasons people have offered for not succeeding. Some are really valid, many are just excuses. To me, that is focusing on the negative. I'd rather look at the question from the other side.

I think the more important question is to analyze what it takes to succeed in a network marketing company. What are the individual skills and activities that give you the strongest probability of success? So let's spend a few minutes looking at:

What Are The Key Factors That Lead To Success In Network Marketing?

There are four significant dynamics that I've observed

that are consistent among those I've met and worked with over the years who have accomplished their goals using the network marketing business model. These are:

First, clearly understanding what success means to them. Not everyone who gets into a network marketing company is looking to achieve the highest rank in the company, or make millions of dollars. We make a mistake assuming they are. I've worked with many people who want to put $500 a month into an education fund for their young children so they can have the opportunity for a college education. Others are looking for $1000 a month from their part time job so they can augment their retirement income. They are not looking to quit their jobs next month. Nor do they want to do the work necessary to become a company leader. They are looking for exactly what a network marketing company can provide: additional income on the side for a modest investment of time and money.

One of the first ways to help a new person is to work with them to understand what will define success for them in this new venture.

Second, there has to be a significant demand for the product or service you're going to be offering. This is the value the marketplace puts on the product, not your opinion. It is important before ever joining a company to evaluate who the potential customer and prospective distributor will be. Do you have experience working with people in those demographics? Are you comfortable doing so...more important, do you enjoy working with them? If your answer is not overwhelmingly positive to these questions, keep searching for another company.

Third, having enough prospects to talk with. You need to have a pool of prospective customers and business associates that you can talk with daily. This is often the most difficult aspect of the business for a new person. The reality is that you must talk with people for them to understand the value of your product and business opportunity.

In recent years I've talked with many distributors who want to rely on social media sites or internet prospecting to build a business. While this can be done, it is a much more difficult process of sifting and sorting than working within the "warm" market that we all have. That warm market is people we already know, and their direct referrals to us.

When you are new to the business, learning the "how to" is much easier when working in your warm market. The reality is that your family and friends will probably not get into business with you, at least not at first. But they will let you "practice" on them so you get competent at presenting your opportunity.

Fourth, understanding the sales cycle. If you were a real estate broker would you expect a new client to immediately purchase the first and only home you showed them? Of course not. There is a decision making process that all of us go through whenever we are considering a large expenditure of time or money. In the case of a network marketing business opportunity, prospective associates are counting the cost of their time, relationships, and the complete investment that will be necessary to reach what they determine is success for them. They are also evaluating you. Do they know-like-trust you enough to associate with you?

All too often we give up because someone asks for more information. "Oh, they weren't interested," we say. In fact, they were just looking for more proof. Make sure you understand all the tools your company offers to help you properly demonstrate to value of your product and opportunity. Keep accurate records as to where you are in the process with each person you are talking with. Once someone comes into your organization take the time to properly orient them to the subtle nuance of this business model and how they can achieve their goals.

Bottom line, this is a people business. The more you can develop your person to person communication skills, the better you will get at bringing customers and associates into your business.

I like network marketing, and have been active in a business for the past five years. I encourage anyone who is considering a secondary source of income to look carefully at network marketing companies with products/services that interest them. Following the steps outlined in this report will help you make a decision that is right for you.

My Four Critical Criteria Use To Evaluate A Network Marketing Company

In the introduction to this book I said that as a part of investigating many network marketing companies for myself and clients, I have developed four additional questions that I consider when evaluating a company in the Network Marketing space.

Since so many people are looking at this business model, particularly for a secondary income, I want to share these with you.

1. Is the company at least 5 years old?

As more and more companies choose network marketing as their business growth strategy, this becomes a key question to ask. Fully 94% of network marketing companies fail in their first five years! There are many reasons for this. Poorly designed compensation plans, not sufficient capital in the company to begin with, a product/service that is not well received in the marketplace, regulatory change (particularly in health/wellness companies), and a myriad of other reasons.

So the first thing I want to see is the age of the company.

There is a prevalent belief about network marketing that only the people who are first in the company make the really big money. These "early adaptors" naturally earn the most because they're closest to the parent company in the genealogy. That is not the case in any well designed compensation plan, and I want to dispel this myth.

If that were true, how do you explain companies like Amway and Shaklee, both are about 50 years old, that are creating new six and seven figure distributor teams every year.

There is no question that a good distributor who is "early" to the party can create great wealth and residual income. But what really drives rapid growth in a network marketing organization is taking advantage of "momentum" waves when they occur. Momentum in this business model is defined as when the distributor and company no longer have to explain who they are and what the product is, but people "on the street" are aware of and looking for the company/product. This initial momentum wave can propel even an average distributor to a level of success they couldn't have imagined when joining the company.

Momentum can also be created when the company opens a new country or region in the world. Remember, even if you don't know anyone in that country, someone on your team, someone a dozen or more levels removed from you that you don't even know, might have extensive relationships in that country and drive a huge surge of business volume.

Another driver of momentum is a new product or line of products being released.

There is a negative corollary to the momentum cycle of a company as well. That occurs when the company "buys" momentum. This is done by going to successful distributors in other companies and paying them an incentive to quit their company and "join" the company seeking to buy momentum. Implied in the purchase is the idea that the distributor will exert their best efforts to get most of their current down line to "move" with them. Think of a "free agent" in the sports world selling themselves to the highest bidding team.

When I see this it is a clear indication that I want nothing to do with that company. First, if a person could be bribed to move once, what is to say they won't be bribed again by another company, again taking their volume with them. More important, if the momentum wave is artificially created it cannot be sustained for too long. Eventually the company will run out of money for bribes or people to bribe.

True "organic" momentum is a quantifiable event—you can see it building like a tsunami in the growth of customers and distributors. And like a tidal wave, it picks up and carries everyone in its path. This is how a newer person in a well designed network marketing company can quickly build a large organization and pass by distributors who were earlier to the game.

2. Can I quantify the results of the product or service?

Whether you are marketing business to business or business to consumer it is important to be able to demonstrate measurable results if you expect your product to have long term viability.

This is a challenge for many of the health and wellness companies. "Take this and you'll feel better," is a difficult sales model to sustain. What if the person doesn't feel better—no repeat business. Or they might feel better, but can that new sense of well being be attributed to your product? Maybe they just have been getting more sleep, or had a great weekend with their spouse, or their boss at the jobsite stopped picking on them, or....you get the idea.

Especially when marketing to business customers, you will need to be able to clearly state the benefits of your product/service, cost justify the investment, and offer testimonials from satisfied users to get the sale. Then you'll need to demonstrate to this new customer the value of the product/service to keep them buying and create the residual income that is the goal of working in the network marketing business space.

3. Do you actually like the product/service, and use it yourself?

This should be obvious, but I'm occasionally surprised by a client who has only looked at what they believe the financial opportunity might be and hasn't even tried the product. What if you don't like the taste? Hard to sample with a prospect when you make a nasty face every time you open the bottle and get a whiff.

Is the product/service congruent with you and your lifestyle? If you're 75 pounds overweight and affiliate with a diet product program will you be able to market the product with credibility? If you've been fired from your last seventeen jobs, collect food stamps, and drive a ten year old beat up car—should you really be in one of the financial services network marketing opportunities?

Look for a product/service that you can use yourself and share with both enthusiasm and credibility.

4. Would I pay the retail price being asked for this product if there were not a business opportunity associated with it?

This is without doubt the most important criteria for me, and here is what I mean by asking this question. Far too often the price of products sold through the network marketing distribution system is inflated so that multiple levels of commissions can be paid. This has two negative effects.

First, it makes it difficult to create a base of satisfied retail customers that are critical to developing a profitable business with long term sustainable residual income. If you are going to build a "walk away" income through network marketing, you must have a strong base of happy and consistent retail customers. This is particularly true in the health/wellness and home consumables sectors.

Many times I see the higher price being "justified" by some exclusive ingredient or proprietary process. Often there is anecdotal evidence of blind people being able to walk again and the lame to see. I wasn't a very good student in high school chemistry, but I did learn that the body does a pretty good job of breaking down what we swallow into usable compounds. Whether it came from deep within the Amazonian rainforest or from a farm in Iowa, once it's reduced to an elemental state so my body can use it, what's the difference? That may be an oversimplification, but show me a better reason for a higher than market price than a secret recipe.

Second, an expensive product creates an incentive to become a non-working distributor. In fact, many companies market their opportunity this way, to their own detriment. The pitch goes something like, "hey, just pay $20 to be a distributor and then you can buy at wholesale. You'll make your $20 back on the second order."

Why is this a problem? It creates a false base of distributors and actually retards company growth. If, as a building distributor looking to create an organization, I begin to put a lot of customers in and call them distributors, then my down line is not truly a producing business asset. I'm investing my time, training, and money in a pool of people who have little or no commitment to my company or product and don't really value the leadership I offer. Customers can easily be distracted by the next "bright shiny object" to come to the market.

On the other hand, a working distributor is really a business associate who has some investment of time and money in their own success and by extension, yours. Likewise, when you empower them through sharing your time and training with them, you are building a relationship and a tangible business asset.

Back to the essential question, what is the retail price of the product in relation to the competition? If it is higher, then I'm not going to be too interested in getting involved with the company. If it is at least on a par with comparable products available in the open market then I'm willing to look further.

What Is My Opinion

As I said earlier, I like network marketing and work in the industry myself at this time. It was not easy to find a company that met my ten criteria shared earlier in this book, and even more difficult when I add these four more specific to network marketing.

If you are looking for a way to create additional, part time or secondary income, network marketing could be the answer. It is a great business model for the person who is willing to work consistently for several years to build an organization and income, with the goal to eventually go "full time" into their network marketing business. It is not a business to leave your current job for, assuming that you will be successful quickly. Very few have been successful making that leap.

With that caveat in mind, I encourage you to consider network marketing as a business model. There are excellent companies who provide good value to their customers and great support to their distributors. Now that you are armed with some of the questions to ask, find a company that meets your goals and needs.

Chapter 15

I SELL THINGS ON THE INTERNET, SO I'M NOT USED TO DRESSING UP

Is Affiliate Marketing the
Right Business For You?

Sometime back in 2008, as I was investigating ways that I might use the internet to create additional income, I found a program called "Affilorama." It was a downloadable course that introduced me to the business of Affiliate Marketing. Looking back on that manual today the strategies it suggested seem quite primitive. Put that in the context of how quickly things change online. Remember how crude internet marketing was just seven years ago? Or how slow working online was before Web 2.0?

I was intrigued with the idea of selling someone else's product through the web and earning a commission for doing so. I wasn't sure about how to set up a landing page, and pay per click advertising was in its infancy, but something about this business model was alluring. One of the members of my BNI networking chapter was a "web designer" so I hired him to help me set up a couple of basic marketing sites and began experimenting.

Those initial attempts eventually led to a business, "Made Simple Press," that sold ebooks written to people interested in carefully defined niche markets. I hired a website person in the Philippines to create each site, and article writers to research and write copy for several content pages for the sites. The goal was to sell the ebook on that subject to those who came to the site. The authors had a new marketing channel for their book, and we earned a commission on each sale.

In introducing the Affiliate Marketing business model, I am sharing some of my own experience as well as that of many other affiliate marketers I have talked with about their business. In this chapter my goal is to help you understand the business model and how it can create significant profits with a minimal investment. It is a business that meets the criteria of the Ten Vital Questions.

Let's begin with a definition. For people who are used to working online in some capacity, Affiliate Marketing is a familiar term. If you are new to the internet marketing space here's a short definition:

Affiliate Marketing is a revenue stream wherein a person, known as an affiliate marketer, is paid a pre set commission for promoting a product, service, or a website that is not their own.

For example, you decide to join the affiliate program for a successful product or service. It could be a book, seminar, kitchen gadget; really anything that is sold on the internet. Let's say that you find a course that helps someone learn basic German that sells for $40 and offers a 25% commission. You refer 100 people over the next month who purchase the course. The owner of the German language program then pays you $10 for each sale (25% commission) X 100 sales = $1000. The best part about Affiliate Marketing is that you've earned this income without having created any kind of product or service of your own!

This means that the Affiliate Marketing opportunity can

be seized by anyone. You don't have to be an inventor or author, all you need is a computer and the ability to create some ads and landing pages. In many cases the owner of the product will even provide you with ads and emails to help you promote their product!

Now that you have a very basic understanding of what Affiliate Marketing is, I want to share several aspects of this business as a way to help you decide if it is one you want to investigate further. There are many books and courses written on this business strategy, my goal is to just open the door so you can see if you want to go further. To do that I'll share the following:

- How to find and join an affiliate program or company
- Choosing products to promote
- The mechanics of tracking, how you get paid
- Some Best Practices of successful affiliate marketers

What Are Affiliate Programs?

If you were to answer an ad or watch a video about affiliate marketing for beginners, here's what you would probably hear. "Go join Clickbank, choose a product from the marketplace in the health, wealth, and happiness section because they convert the best, and then join my course and I'll tell you how to master the steps to affiliate wealth."

They advise this plan of action because they are selling a training program, and if you are new to the world of affiliate marketing this might seem like a logical course of action. Unfortunately, and I speak from personal experience, the learning curve with this plan is quite steep and can be both discouraging and frustrating. You have to learn how to find the right niche, choose keywords, write copy, build a website, and then drive traffic to the website. Once you have these steps down, then you must split test your ads, headlines, photos, even body copy to constantly find the best combination to increase your sales and profits.

That doesn't begin to consider the high level of competition in these popular niches. Since they can be so lucrative it is not unusual to have several super affiliates who have been in the market for years and have finely tuned marketing machines selling multiple products for them each month. You can make money, but it can be a slow road with a lot of detours until you feel competent.

My caution is not about Clickbank, I have a Clickbank account and have sold my own products through their platform, as well as been an affiliate marketer for others. What I want you to be aware of is that in the affiliate marketing space there are a lot of promoters selling their courses, most promising a quick path to a five figure monthly income. While earning at that level is very realistic for an affiliate marketer, it does not come quickly and there can be a steep learning curve to get to that level.

That being said, I encourage someone considering a business as an affiliate marketer to join several affiliate programs. Let me define what an affiliate program is, and then suggest several you should investigate.

Simply put, affiliate programs are arrangements in which an online merchant website pays affiliate websites a commission to send them traffic. The affiliate website post links to the merchant site and are paid according to an agreed upon formula. This payment agreement is typically based on the number of people the affiliate sends to the merchant's site, or the number of people they send who buy something or perform some other action. These actions can be further defined, but the bottom line is that when the affiliate marketer sends someone to the merchant site he/she gets paid.

There are at least three parties in an affiliate program transaction:

- The customer
- The affiliate site
- The merchant site

The pioneer of this business model was Jeff Bezos, CEO and founder of Amazon.com. All the way back in the late 1990's, the Internet "stone age," he invited people to join Amazon as affiliates and post links to books in return for a percentage of the sale profits. With over 500,000 affiliate websites now promoting products on Amazon this program has been a huge success.

I've now mentioned two of the top affiliate marketing companies based on surveys of participants completed in early 2014. Clickbank was ranked #8, and only sells information products. Amazon was #6 and seems to be selling about everything. Here are the others, listed in the order as ranked by participants:

1. Commission Junction

2. LinkShare

3. one Network Direct

4. ShareASale

5. Plimus

6. Amazon Associates

7. FlexOffers

8. Clickbank

9. Commission Soup

If you are thinking about affiliate marketing as a business, or even to create a second income, I encourage you to visit each of these sites and learn what type of products they typically offer, the merchants that work through them, and any requirements they might have to be an affiliate.

While you can also find individual companies who offer affiliate programs, my suggestion for the person getting started in this business is to choose one of more of these top tier companies as your first step. You'll find a tremendous variety of merchants and products to choose from, many of whom will also provide you with marketing tools so that you can be successful faster.

The process of becoming an affiliate is quite simple. Go to their site and complete an online application to become a member. The application will ask for some general personal information, and data about your website (URL, name, and description of content.) If you don't yet have a website with traffic some affiliate networks will not let you register until you do. Others recognize that you are looking for a product to promote and will be building a site to accomplish that. You will have to agree to their Terms of Service. Most of the affiliate networks are free for affiliates.

Once approved you can begin picking products that interest you. In some cases the merchant offering the product/service will want to know more about you and your site, and may want to approve you as an affiliate. This is not typical, but can happen.

Either the merchant or the affiliate network will also establish payment terms with you. Since the transaction size is generally quite small, they will establish a minimum threshold of earnings before they send you a check.

Identifying Products to Market

Now the fun part--what are you going to offer to the marketplace? I've seen more than one person make this choice based on what seems to be selling well as they analyze the statistics provided by the affiliate network. This is generally a mistake. If you aren't familiar with the product or the market the product is designed to serve you will have a difficult time creating a believable website to promote it. Just because something is selling well for another affiliate doesn't guarantee your success.

A better selection method is to identify some categories of products that you have used, know something about, and can speak with some authority about. Then go into the affiliate networks and search for products in these categories. You'll be far more effective as a marketer and over time sell more when the copy on your website conveys your own feelings about the product.

A common question from new affiliate marketers is, "how many products can I market?" The simple answer is, "as many as you want." While it is true that there is no limit to the number of products or services you can build a landing page or website and promote, a 'best practice' is to begin with no more than three.

The reason for this is the learning curve that is a part of marketing online. I'm not talking about the technical aspects of website design or programming languages. Building a new website is actually one of the easiest parts of your marketing plan. There are numerous "templates" where you can literally drag and drop graphics and text boxes and have a site up in minutes.

What is less obvious is how to design and build a successful sales funnel to drive qualified traffic to your new site. Pay per click or banner ads? Which headline is most effective? What color should the Buy Now button be? Do I need a full website, or just a landing page? Can I get traffic for this offer by using a CPA network?

Learning the subtle nuances of capturing a market for the product you want to promote will occupy most of your time. Truthfully, it is an activity that will never stop as long as you are in this business. Until you develop a competency in driving traffic to a site it will do you no good to keep building more sites. Which is why I encourage you to find three or fewer related products and then concentrate on learning the skill of attracting people to your sites.

The Mechanics of Tracking Affiliate Links--How You Get Paid!

You've found a product you like and are excited about promoting. You build a great website filled with information designed to help someone make a buying decision. Even more important, the banner ads you designed are bringing people to your site every day. When one of these prospects clicks on your "Buy Now" button, how does the merchant know it was your good work that brought them the sale? How do they know to pay you?

The connections that make affiliate marketing work are called "links." There are several types of links and you might use more than one in a campaign. Each type is specially suited for particular purpose. Some common link types include:

- Text Links. When you are reading copy on a web page and there is a phrase that is typically in blue type and underlined, then you have just read a Text Link. If you click on that text your browser will automatically bring up the related webpage. The advantage of text links in an affiliate program is that they are ingrained in the content of your site so don't look like an advertisement. For many affiliate sites this is the most natural way to link to the merchant site.

- Banner Links. These links appear as boxes, usually containing words and a graphic element. They may be the best choice when you think a text link doesn't do enough to attract visitors.
- Search box. This type of link allows visitors to search an online database on another sites. The results of the search are links to other pages on the site.

Affiliate programs use these links in several ways:

- Link to the home page. This is a straight forward link to the merchant's home page. If an affiliate wants to introduce visitors to the merchant site in general, this is the best way to link.
- Product specific link. If an affiliate website wants to sell only a specific product, they can link to that products page on the merchant website. This makes things easier for the customer and simplifies the affiliate program process.
- Storefronts. If an affiliate website wants to expose visitors to a variety of products, they can link to a storefront. These storefronts are maintained by the merchant website. The merchant can change what products are on

display, but keeps the URL the same so the affiliate doesn't have to change any coding. Some merchants also maintain storefront pages the affiliate can customize so that they display the most relevant products.

- Co-Branding. In some affiliate programs, affiliates can maintain their website identity after a customer links to the merchant website. The merchant website will handle all the sales, and will usually host the page, but will configure the page so that it appears as though it's still part of the affiliate website. Unless the user examines the URL displayed by his browse he won't know he's has linked to another site.

- Registration. An affiliate can link directly to a registration form on the merchant site. If a visitor would have to register to use the merchant's website, this link is a good time saver.

Putting All This Technology Together

How do affiliate networks know when a visitor clicks from an affiliate to the merchant site? In most cases the answer is that the visitor doesn't actually go directly to the merchant site, but to a page on the affiliate network site. The URL for that page contains several pieces of information, including:

- An identification number for the affiliate
- An identification number for the merchant
- The URL of the merchant site

When you click on the link, the network site records a hit on that particular URL, which tells them what affiliate sent a visitor to that merchant. It then immediately sends the visitor to the actual merchant site. This happens so quickly that you never see any hint of the network in your browser window. If you were to move your pointer over a merchant link on an affiliate site you will notice that the first part of the URL your browser displays is for the network site and not for the merchant.

The network tracks sales using Internet cookies containing these same identification numbers, allowing them to keep track of what affiliate referred the customer to the merchant.

3 Types of Affiliate Marketers

One of the appeals of affiliate marketing is that you don't have to create a product. You can literally find something that looks interesting, become an affiliate for the product, and promote it. If you are a good marketer and can attract traffic to your site you will make money. If this was your strategy, you would be considered an "unattached" affiliate marketer.

One of the ways to categorize how people earn money as affiliates is the level of involvement they have with the product being offered. There are three groups: unattached, related, and involved.

Unattached affiliate marketing campaigns are typically pay per click or banner ad strategies where you as the marketer have no presence and no authority in the niche of the product you are promoting. There is no connection between you and the end consumer. All you are doing is putting an affiliate link in front of people and hoping they click on it, earning you a commission.

This is often how someone gets started in affiliate marketing. If you don't have a website or blog with followers, or a list of people you can promote to, it may be the only option. The challenge with staying in this strategic position long term is that it is really not a business model that creates sustainable income without your constant involvement. Essentially you are a behind the scenes middle man buying ad space on line.

The second group is what I refer to as related affiliate marketing. This describes the person who has a website or blog and has created a presence in the online world in one or more niches. They might also have a podcast or series of videos, and make a conscious effort to attract a following of other like minded individuals. The related affiliate marketer will allow affiliate links to be put on their site for products that are related to their niche. They may or may not use these products, or know too much about them. Since they have some connection with the niche subject, it is hoped that visitors to the site will click on these links.

The last group is the involved affiliate marketer. As you might guess, this is where the person promoting the product or service has used it personally and believes in it. Their recommendation is based on their own experience. It is this personal involvement with the product that makes the offer more attractive.

There is not a hierarchy here--one style of affiliate marketing is not better than the others. Many times though, there is a progression. Someone will start out as an unattached marketer just to begin their business. As they become more proficient on line, and develop their own web properties and followers, they begin to offer related products. Over time, as their interests become more defined, they may choose to focus on products they are truly involved with. Most affiliate marketers that I've met who have been online for a length of time and have developed an expertise in their business do a little bit of each style. They will tell you that the most profitable products are those they promote where they are involved with the product and really understand the people who might want to buy it.

Six Affiliate Marketing Best Practices

Success leaves clues, and in the field of affiliate marketing there are consistent actions that the highest income earners have in common. Here are six of them:

1. When researching affiliate companies and programs make sure you understand their commission rates, payout points, return policy and customer service practices. Ideally you will find multiple products you are interested in within one company.

2. One of your primary objectives is to build a list of names and email addresses you control. That allows you to go back to those who purchased from you with new, related products or services. Never send a customer directly to a vendor's site unless you have gotten their info first.

3. Take the time to set up your own website or blog. This will help you brand yourself as a marketer and someone with experience/expertise in the niche. By having your own site you now have a platform to publish reviews, information, and product tips.

4. Research your prospective customers. Understand the demographics of the people who might buy what you are offering. Who are they? Age? Gender? Economic status? Education? Knowing this allows you

to "talk" with them on your site or in your blog. They'll come to trust you as an advisor and not just a marketer.

5. As you build your list and site reputation, offer your visitors free reports that provide valuable information on your niche. Inside the report you can include your affiliate links.

6. Only recommend good products. It isn't just the merchant's reputation that is on the line. If you intend to build a highly profitable affiliate marketing business you must focus on consistently offering good value.

What Is My Opinion:

Affiliate marketing is possibly the most popular way to make money online. It has the allure of high income potential, but is too often touted as being a simple business model. "All you need is a computer" is how the ads read. It is not always that easy though, it is important to know how to become a good affiliate and why you should promote the right content, to the right people.

Getting into the affiliate marketing business is quite simple, becoming competent and highly profitable requires a learning curve. You will have to become proficient with several software packages, web design, copywriting, designing ads, and marketing funnels. None of this is overwhelming, but if your goal is to make a significant income over time you will have to master each of these tasks. Many can be delegated to a virtual assistant as you grow your business.

This is also a business where you can literally never leave your computer or talk with someone in person. Since the entire business is conducted online, there is not a lot of social interaction. You will need a high degree of self discipline to stay focused on the tasks that must be done each day. If you are a more social person who likes to work in a group or have regular contact with others, affiliate marketing will not be a good fit for you.

Once you understand those potential negatives, if you are confident you can overcome them then the affiliate marketing business could be what you are looking for. It is another of the business models that can be started part time, allowing you to transition when the business grows enough to support your needs. It does not require a lot of initial capital, and once you have developed your pattern of management you can delegate many of the more repetitive tasks. Over time you can have a product funnel producing regular income with very little input from you.

Which is why I've included Affiliate Marketing as a business model for you to consider.

Chapter 16

THE CONSULTANTS WE BROUGHT IN TO MONITOR THE CONSULTANTS
WHO ARE LOOKING INTO OUR CUTTING BACK ON CONSULTANTS ARE
RECOMMENDING SPECIALIST CONSULTANTS

Consulting: Are You Ready to Translate Your Expertise Into A Career?

There is often a level of confusion that surrounds the title "Consultant." For many who have worked in a larger corporate setting, the Consultant is someone from the outside who is not familiar with 'how things are done around here,' and who typically wants to make a lot of changes. Others have experienced working with a consultant on specific, short term projects; and assume that is what a consultant does. Occasionally an organization will call in a consultant to act as an Interim Manager or Executive for a specific period of time.

In fact, all of these are a correct understanding of what a consultant does.

The role of consultant is not limited to corporate or business applications. It is common to find "consultants" in many fields: security, personal health, copywriting, wedding planning, jury selection and literally dozens more. Essentially, being a consultant involves giving expert advice in a particular field. In offering your services as a consultant, you are indicating that you have a wide knowledge of your area of specialization, and can effectively communicate that knowledge and experience to your client and their team.

A properly designed and established consulting business fits the criteria of the Ten Vital Questions. As you know if you've read this far, I work as a marketing and business growth consultant today. It can be rewarding and lucrative career.

In this overview of consulting as a business model, I'm going to touch on several aspects of creating and building a consulting practice. This is not intended to be an exhaustive study on how to create a successful consultancy. Instead, I want to give you enough information to decide if this career is something you should consider looking into further. Here's what I want to cover:

- What I see as the 'reality' of consulting
- Why companies hire consultants
- A "day in the life" of a consultant
- The importance of specializing
- How to brand your consulting practice
- Pricing strategies
- Getting and keeping clients

Please keep in mind that my personal experience for the past eleven years is working with companies on their marketing and business growth strategies. That is my area of expertise. Your specialty is most likely in another area. With that in mind I am going to avoid specific examples about my business, trying to share more general information about the consulting profession.

Throughout this chapter I am speaking to the person considering starting a consulting business that they will own and do most of the 'hands on' work. In doing so I'm making an assumption that this person has been working in the area that they will be consulting in for a considerable period of time. They may have owned a business in the field, worked in a senior position for a large company, or been a university faculty member teaching the subject. The majority of consultants that I have known and worked with came to the profession as a second career. They've "paid their dues" and are now ready to capitalize on the knowledge and expertise developed during their working life. Often they have been "downsized" from a corporate management position, or take an early retirement.

The alternative to starting a consultancy is to become a "staff consultant" with one of the large consulting firms that contract with national and multi-national firms. This is typically a position that appeals to recent graduates with an undergraduate or masters degree in the field they'll be consulting in. These firms have established protocols that their staff consultants follow for each client company. It is a great 'early career' move to gain a wide breadth of knowledge and build contacts in the field. The person who chooses this path will be an employee of the consulting firm, and thus not who I am writing this chapter for.

There are two aspects of the consulting business that I will go into more detail on. First, pricing and various strategies for pricing you services. Second, how to identify prospective clients and retain their business. In talking with other active consultants, and those who are investigating a career as a consultant, these are the two areas that create the most questions.

What is The Reality of Consulting?

Consulting can be a tremendously satisfying profession, as well as a lucrative one. Analyzing the current situation faced by your client, helping them determine where they want to go, and then designing a solution that is implemented and achieves the desired result is extremely fulfilling. As you develop your individual methods and style, and build a reputation for success in your field of expertise, you will be able to earn a significant financial return for your time invested.

There are several aspects of the consulting business that can lead to an excellent quality of life. Some of these include:

1. Flexibility

You can completely control your schedule; getting up any time you choose in the morning, and taking time off when you want. Your schedule is whatever you make of it.

There is a caveat to all of this flexibility, call it a big myth about consulting. Many people will make it seem you can enjoy this kind of relaxed schedule from day one. The problem is they are only telling you part of the story. While you will have total discretion as to when you work and when you don't– in reality to be successful in this business takes a lot of hard work.

Depending on the type of client you are working with, there may be non-negotiable periods of time when you must be focused on their business, or even working in their offices. The number of client projects you accept will also determine how much time you can afford to take off and still meet project objectives. I do not know a single person who is successful as a consultant who didn't put in long hours the first couple years they were building their business.

Be clear on this, there is huge room for flexibility and being in control of your own schedule...but it takes a lot of hard work to get to that place in your business.

2. You can choose who you work with

We've all had to pleasure at one time or another of working with a bunch of bozos. They're annoying, they make promises and don't follow through, they miss deadlines, tell long and pointless stories in the middle of meetings...the list goes on. Maybe they were your boss, or another employee. Whatever.

When you're a consultant you choose who you want to work with. You can take on projects that interest you and that you want to work on, and not worry about the rest. There is plenty of room in most consulting markets for you to pick and choose what you work on.

3. You Have Control Over Your Income

There's only one person who can control what you earn – that's you! Even in the early stages of your practice, when you are a solopreneur, you really can earn as much or as little as you want in this business. If you want to make $50,000-$60,000 working part-time or $100,000+ a year you can do it. If you choose to leverage your time and expertise by hiring sales people and a 'back office' fulfillment team you can create a sizeable business only limited by how large you want to grow.

You shouldn't expect to reach this level overnight. Just as with any business, you must create a business plan and determine what you want your consultancy to be, and the timeline to achieve those goals. Understanding the metrics of your business, and installing systems to monitor your progress in each area will enable you to create a business that provides the quality of life your dreamed of when starting out.

There are two sides to every coin, and the consulting profession has it's unique challenges. These include:

1. The emotional difference from a "job"

As consultants we constantly battle loneliness, determination, and must deal with self motivation. This may sound like an insignificant challenge, you may be saying "that's not a problem for me at all." You may be right and are an exception to what is a common situation for consultants. Until you dedicate all your time to being a consultant, you'll never really know how prepared you are for this.

The fact is most consultants work alone, at least in the early days. A great deal of them work from a home office, which makes good economic sense, but can be isolating. You will be spending a lot of time by yourself, and need to be emotionally prepared for what comes with the territory.

You will feel lonely. You'll be sitting in your office, staring at your computer or a piece of paper and you'll have no one to talk with. You'll have distractions all around you. TV, surfing the web, playing with the dog, to whatever else you can find to take your mind away from your work. If you have a spouse or children at home during some or all of your workday it can be challenging to help them understand that you are "working" even though you are at home.

One of the greatest characteristics that a consultant must possess is self motivation. You won't have a "boss" directing your actions each day, so must be able to motivate yourself. There will definitely come days when you question why you ever decided to become a consultant. You'll ask yourself should you really be in this position where you have no stable income, have to constantly please clients who often don't understand or appreciate what you're trying to do for them, and have no one to regularly talk with throughout the day. On days like that, it is your daily and weekly goals that will help you stay focused.

For my own business I have developed several routines that help me stay on track. For example, I have two regularly scheduled conversations each week with other consultants. They have a different area of expertise, so we think of each other as colleagues and not competitors. We can compare experiences, talk about our projects, and our frustrations. Just the action of being able to vent to another like minded professional helps me.

I also strive to schedule any face to face meetings that will take me out of the office on Wednesdays. I do this for two reasons. One is effective time management--I cut down on travel time and don't interrupt valuable working time blocks by "going to a meeting." By scheduling these on a Wednesday it breaks up my week. I find myself recharged and ready to complete any deadlines by the end of the day on Friday.

2. Client Issues

There is no escaping dealing with client issues. No matter how carefully pick your clients, and if you only take on projects that you are most interested in...without a doubt there will be times when something goes wrong. It usually is unexpected and can be a shock your system. Maybe the work that you thought would improve your clients' business hasn't worked as they expected, and they want answers.

Perhaps a couple of client checks are late and you struggle with confronting them over their bill paying practices.

No matter how experienced and knowledgeable you are, you will make a mistake from time to time, and have to find a way to both correct the error and make sure your client stays happy.

If you grow your practice to the point where you have employees, it a certainty that a client will get upset over something one of them says or does.

What I want you to understand now, as you are considering a consulting business, is that you WILL have client issues. When they happen it can be incredibly discouraging. It is easy to get down on yourself and wonder if you made a mistake choosing this business. An interesting facet of the consulting life is that it can be like riding a roller coaster. There will be many thrilling ups, but you'll also experience the occasional downs.

3. Can I make some real money?

The short answer is yes, you can. If you remember just a moment ago I pointed out that you have control over your income. That is true, you that you can make very stable income as a consultant. The idea that working a

9-5 JOB is more stable than being a consultant is largely a myth.

As a consultant, you control how many clients you work with at any one time. Some work with just one a year, others work with 10 or more. Doing this allows you to keep yourself protected, so even if one client ends your engagement with them, you'll still have income from the others.

There are two types of agreements that most consultants structure with their clients. First is the specific project. This might be helping them get ready for a trade show, or building a series of letters to be sent to their customer list, or any sort of "one off" project where they ask for your help. You quote them a fee for the specific tasks to be done, and when finished that is the end.

The second is an ongoing retainer based consulting relationship. In this case you might agree to produce three YouTube videos a month for the next year, or manage the details of a quarterly meeting of all of your clients sales staff for the next two years. Whatever the task, it is repeated for a pre-determined period of time.

My recommendation is that you strive for a balance of both. The specific project clients are, for me, great fun. I help define the scope of the project, and then execute the solution we've agreed on. The fees are typically higher, and these days are a nice break from the routine of managing a group of clients who all have different, ongoing needs.

The balance is that the longer term consulting agreements provide stability to your practice. You know that you will be working for a client over time, you get to know them far more intimately, and can enjoy seeing the fruits of your expertise in their success. These relationships also provide stable cash flow, a critical component of any consulting business.

In the beginning you will also be devoting a percentage of your time to marketing your own business, meeting with prospective clients, and developing proposals. No matter how many clients you have, this activity never stops. You may delegate to a sales team at some future time, but as the business owner you will always want to be involved in the development of new clients.

Just like any other business you might consider, a consulting practice has a great number of alluring qualities. Of course, just like any other business, there are some challenges you will face. After eleven years in this profession I believe that the positive aspects of the career outweigh the negative.

Why Do Companies Hire Consultants?

If you have never worked with a consultant in the past, your first question as you consider this business model might be along the lines of, "why would someone hire a consultant?" There are quite a few really good reasons a company considers bringing in a specialist. Here are just a few of them:

- Consultant add experience from their work with other related companies
- Consultants add more brains to a problem, increasing the chances of finding a solution
- Consultants do the research and analytical work that you don't have time or resources for
- Consultants represent an outside viewpoint-- someone who can look at a problem without a personal stake in the company's politics
- Consultants may have particular expertise that the client doesn't have

An unspoken question in the mind of many thinking about consulting is more personal, "why would someone hire *me* as a consultant?" Look at the reasons I've just listed and apply them to your career history and area of expertise. There are certainly some areas of knowledge that you have considerable experience in. That can be a real value to another business owner. Your years of experience provide you with an ability to quickly discern the challenges a company might be facing, and offer advice based on that experience. You are a "fresh set of eyes" looking at a situation.

Companies hire consultants, and will hire *you*, for all of these reasons.

A Day in the Life of a Consultant

OK, I've given myself this new title: consultant. I even have a business card with my new company name and phone number. What do I do every day?

Everyone has different schedules, so to tell you that I know how the typical consultant manages their day would be foolish. I'll briefly share how I schedule my time, but only with the caveat that this works for me and is not necessarily what will help you become successful. Of more value will be to give you a list of many of the activities you do as a consultant and let you visualize how you might balance them, which I will also do.

My schedule is pretty consistent, intentionally so. I'm one of those morning people whose feet hit the floor between 5:30 and 6:00 AM, ready to go. I have an office in my home, and typically will grab a bottle of water and head for my computer. I work until about 8, primarily focusing on personal study time more than client business.

I'll make a protein shake for breakfast, feed my dog, and relax for a few minutes.

The morning hours are my most productive, so I'm back to the computer by 8:30 working on client projects or writing. I take a break at 10, and then get back and try to complete whatever my project goal was for the morning.

After lunch I'll work on business that requires a little less concentration, research or client reports, that kind of thing. I typically stop between 5 and 5:30 in the afternoon, relax a little and have dinner. After dinner I'll work for something less than an hour. Typically this time is focused on a last minute details that needed to be finished for the day, and plan my schedule for the following day.

I mentioned earlier that I typically try to book "out of the office" appointments on Wednesday. That doesn't always work for my clients or prospects, so I will set up meetings on another afternoon as necessary. I never take a breakfast meeting, and rarely a business lunch.

Prospecting for new business and initial meetings with prospective clients can typically be scheduled in the afternoon, and that's what I strive to do. I also try to schedule telephone conversations in the afternoon. I am a member of a Master Mind group of six marketing consultants. We are all in different parts of the US and Canada, and meet by telephone for two hours every Monday evening.

I used to work a lot on Saturday, less so now.

Again let me say that this routine works for me. If you have a body clock that allows you to be productive at 9 PM yours will be different.

Instead of suggesting a daily routine, let me point out some of the time and business management issues you'll encounter as a consultant. These are based on my personal experience, as well as that of others I know in the industry, and are not in any particular order. Some I'll phrase as questions and encourage you to reflect on them.

1. What are your financial/quality of life goals for this business? Many consultants work with a small number of clients, spend 20 to 30 hours a week on their business, and that is all they want. Others are looking to build a larger enterprise, eventually hiring sales and fulfillment teams, and will work the 50 hours a week that requires. Others plan a four day work week, still others work three weeks a month only. The point here is that you want to spend some time thinking about work/life balance.

2. What is your optimal "time block." By time block I mean what is the length of time that you can effectively concentrate on a task. Mine is 90 minutes, and I schedule my mornings into three time blocks of this length. For you it may be more or less, but it is an important number to know. As you build a base of clients you will be concentrating on specific activities on their behalf. Knowing your effective time block will help you manage a diverse load of clients and actions as you will schedule your time for maximum productivity.

3. How will you prospect for new clients? Do you belong to networking groups, professional organizations, or a Chamber of Commerce? When are the meetings? Book them into your week, and don't forget travel time. In the early years of my business I joined a local chapter of Business Network International (BNI). I knew that every Wednesday we met for lunch, and it was a two and a half hour time commitment including travel.

4. What ongoing training will you be pursuing? Can you do this on-line, or do you have to go to a conference or event? Several times a month I log into web based training and user group sessions for some of the software programs I use in my business. These are typically scheduled far enough in advance to enable you to plan for them.

5. What other personal and family obligations do you have? One of the real advantages of being a consultant is that you have control over your time. If you want to pick your kids up at school and spend an hour with them in the afternoon you have that flexibility.

I hope that you are beginning to realize that there is not a typical "day in the life" of a consultant. Your typical day will be what you design it to be. That is one of the beauties of this profession.

Consult with a Rifle, not a Shotgun

I was going to title this section something about the

importance of being a specialist in your consulting practice, but that was boring. I like the image of the rifle vs. the shotgun. Here's what I mean: What do you do better than anyone else? Or more likely, ask yourself what you do better than most people? What is your area of expertise? What do people ask your advice and opinion on? Whatever that is, that's probably the area of consulting you should be in. It is highly focused--like a rifle.

The alternative is to try and do a wide variety of activities for a diversity of clients. This is more than just difficult to do. This style of business will make your marketing far more difficult, and limit the referral business you'll receive. Dan Kennedy has a saying that I like: "If everyone is your customer, no one is your customer." It's true.

If you're continuing to read this chapter, I suspect that by now you've likely got some ideas about what kind of consultant you want to be, so I won't spend time on that. I will encourage you to be sure that you have a passion for and are interested in the area of consulting you have chosen. If you were bored with what you did in a corporate job, becoming a consultant for the same niche specialty is not going to change that.

Let me speak a little bit more to this issue of specialization. When people ask what I do, I can easily say I'm a Marketing Consultant. That is accurate. Now think for a minute how many people do you know in some type of marketing? Quite a few would be my guess. The problem with taking a general approach is that you get lost in the mix. There is nothing to make you stand out. That makes hiring you a more difficult decision for your client and people that would potentially refer you to someone they know.

A better approach to take is to specialize. For example, if you go to our website, www.TheAlchemyConsultingGroup.com you'll see that our value proposition, stated clearly at the top of the home page, is: Our Business is Getting You Profitable Sales Leads In Real Time. There are two key words in that statement: 'Profitable' and 'Real Time.' Profitable certainly catches the attention of a prospective client, every business owner wants to be profitable. And Real Time creates curiosity, what exactly does that mean?

The sub-heading has been crafted with equal precision: *"Using a Unique Modular Approach to Marketing and Business Growth, we can Identify and Profitably Convert Prospects into Customers for any Company, Product, or Service"*

It immediately prompts thoughts/questions in the mind of the reader. "What is a modular approach?" "Identify and profitably convert...I like that profitably convert term." "Any company, product, or service...really? How do they do that?"

If I just say I'm a marketing consultant that doesn't really convey what I do.

A Myth About Focus

Many consultants are scared to position themselves as specialists and focus on one specific area. They think that if they do this, they will be turning away a great deal of business. This is a common attitude with the business owners we consult with, and is a logical question for you to be asking too.

What I can tell you is without a doubt, specializing and focusing your services is the way to go. Clients are looking to hire someone when they have a specific need and if you can position yourself to fill that need with your specialization, and offer a compelling value proposition, you have a good chance to be selected.

Here's my suggestion. Choose one area that you can really specialize in. Make
that the focus of your efforts. Your website and marketing materials, even your elevator pitch, should communicate your specialty and value proposition.
As soon as you start focusing you will see potential clients and people that you talk to open up, they will be much more interested in your area of expertise than they would be in general skills.

Think of a wedding photographer. There are many wedding photographers that earn an amazing income. They charge $5000 plus for a couple days work. That same photographer, if they marketed themselves as a general photographer that also does wedding photos, would not be anywhere near as successful. Nobody wants a generalist when they have a specific need in mind.

With that said, there is a second part to this myth. Just because you are focusing your services on one area of specialty, it doesn't mean you can't help your client with other areas as they come up. While we market our company as providing several services focused on generating profitable sales leads; it is rare that we are not also asked to help identify operational issues, train employees, or write updates to their business plan.

The truth is this is a typical experience, and the reason is simple. Once they have become a client and see that you can help them, they will undoubtedly pass you more and more work because they are comfortable with you and trust you.

So pick your focus, communicate it effectively, and watch the opportunities begin.

The Most Lucrative Areas of Consulting

I'm sure you are well aware there are all kinds of consultants in the market place. That should assure you that you can make a very good living in almost any area of consulting. Becoming a certain kind of consultant because you think it has bigger income potential is a bad move. You'll most likely become unhappy as you won't be as passionate about the work. Becoming a successful consultant involves on-going education and training, you don't want to be studying and learning about something that bores you.

That said, here are some points to consider in order to find the optimum combination of work you'll enjoy that will also pay well.

1) Can you demonstrate results?
You need to be able to demonstrate results. If the product that you deliver isn't visible and can't be measured in one form or another, you're not in a lucrative business. The reason is clients want to see results. They need to justify paying you. And if they can't see improvements, they have no reason to cough up the cash for you.

So be sure that whatever it is you are doing for your clients, that you have established a clear goal that is meaningful to both you and the client's business.

This could be increased sales, more leads, decreased costs, improved satisfaction rates, improved manufacturing speed...you get the point. Make sure the work you do can be linked to results. By far, this is the most important weapon in a consultant's arsenal. When push comes to shove, the consultant that has shown they can deliver results will always land new projects and keep existing ones longer than someone that can't demonstrate results.

What I want to stress here is that you don't need to be a magician. It's not necessary to move mountains with your results, and your clients aren't expecting you to do so. The key to keeping your clients happy with your work is to establish clear and regular goals with them. Make sure that your client sees the value in the goal you've agreed on. It should be obvious, but make the goal something that you are confident you can accomplish. Promising something you can't deliver is a quick way to earn a bad reputation and end your work with that client. There's nothing wrong with gradual improvements – as long as that's what you and your client have agreed to.

2) Keep the work going

I spoke earlier about having a balance between "one off" clients who just retain you for a specific job and those clients who keep you on a monthly retainer. You will create a more stable consultancy if you have several clients who pay you monthly. Now that you're showing your clients results, they have the incentive to continue paying you and giving you more work.

To make the consulting business lucrative you need to ensure that you've shown your clients a clear path and plan on how you will continually help them to improve their business and get results. This gives you a solid foundation. Instead of a $1000 project, the client can be worth $12,000 to you as you work with them over the year.

Your plan should show your overall process, and how when you do A for the client successfully, you can then work on B, and then C. Don't worry so much about sticking to this plan rigidly. Nothing goes in a straight line. Your clients' business will change, their priorities will change. As long as you're there doing good work they will continually call on you for help.

3) Fish in the Right Stream

A lucrative consulting business is also one that is in a hungry market. Even if you generate the best of results, if there aren't many people that want what you offer you can't build a solid business. You have to be "fishing" where there are fish to catch.

The current focus for many consultants is niche businesses. That is, finding a specific business category, becoming an expert in that business, and offering your services to business owners in the niche. We do this in our business. We have developed an expertise in helping companies in three niches grow their business: roofing contractors, moving companies, and professional practices. That doesn't mean we won't work in another market, but the focus of our business marketing is primarily in these three niches. I talked about this strategy back in Chapter 9.

The other issue to consider is the severity of the need you will be filling. The

more difficult a client perceives your work to be the more they will be willing
to pay. Do a market analysis and see what the need is for the services you offer. Generally, if there are many other consultants in that area, or businesses that offer the kinds of services that you do, it means there is strong market opportunity.

Even in a crowded marketplace, the skillful consultant will find a way to stand out and become a sought after advisor.

How to Brand Your Consulting Practice

You have probably heard of the 80/20 rule. It's actually called Pareto's Principle after the Italian mathematician by that name. Applying Pareto to the consulting business, you would conclude that 20% of the consultants in any given market will generate 80% of the business. That means that the other 80% are fighting over the remaining 20%. This principle holds true in many fields. Look at real estate agents. The top 20% have sales and incomes far higher than the others in their market.

How can you become one of those consultants in the top 20%? First you need to stand out. If no one can find you, you're not going to get any significant business.

1) Market yourself so that people can find you.

Your challenge as a new consultant is going to be getting found by your target market. You can get out and network, put targeted ads online and in trade publications, do article writing, and much more. Marketing your services is a critical aspect of every consultant's business. There are several ways to do this:

a) Create a consistent brand

The name, logo, color palate, forms you use, email header, unique selling proposition--all of the ways that someone can come into contact with your firm must be consistent. How the phones are answered, your afterhours voicemail, labels you put on proposal packages all must convey the image of a professional business that pays attention to detail. The key for the solopreneur is to invest the time, thought, and money in this process when starting the business.

b) Pricing strategy

You can charge much lower than your competition (never a good model!!) or charge much higher; as long as you're providing more value and people are willing to pay for it.

One of the reasons we chose to go to the market with what we call our "Modular Approach" is that it allows us to break out individual services at various price points depending on the clients need an budget. We state that very clearly on the home page of our web site.

c) Your guarantee

It takes confidence in your services to offer clients a guarantee. For instance, I offer my clients a guarantee that they will see the results we've agreed on, and if they aren't happy, I will continue to work with them at no cost until those results are achieved. Not many people are willing to do this. If you are, you'll instantly pique the interest of prospective clients.

d) Professional communication

Be professional. It's unbelievable how many consultants call themselves professional and yet they fail to return their clients calls on time and follow through as they promised they would. If you take action right away, communicate and act like a real professional, people will take notice. This builds a level of trust with your clients. When you're delivering results and are dependable your clients will have little reason to give their business to anyone else.

e) Make it easy to contact you

It's not uncommon for a potential client to give you a call or send you an email when they feel they might need one of the services you provide. When this happens, if you don't reply in a reasonable time, or it is difficult for a prospect to get in touch with you (no voicemail or no easy way to make contact) you can pretty much kiss that business good bye. Business owners don't have the time or patience to try repeatedly to get in touch with you. If you don't make it easy, they simply won't.

Pricing Strategies

As I said at the beginning of this chapter, I'm going to give you a lot of information about how to price your services. This is, for all new to the consulting business, a challenge in the early days of your practice.

There are several ways you can determine how to set your consulting rates and fees.
There really is no right or wrong way to go about this, as long as the result has you getting paid what you feel is fair and that your fees give you enough cash flow to sustain and grow your business.

The worst thing you can do as a consultant is undercharge. The only possible exception here is if you have just opened your practice and want to get a few client projects working. In that case, taking on some lower paying work to establish yourself, build a client list, and prove your skills is a smart move.

The danger in undercharging is that clients will naturally undervalue your services. In general, the more you charge, the greater the perception clients will have of the value of your services. Of course, the negative corollary to this is that no matter how much they perceive value in what you offer, if they can't afford it you won't get the job.

Let me describe the two methods for determining how to charge for your work that I've seen in practice. First is the simple competitive market analysis. I talk extensively about this in Chapter 8 so won't repeat myself. Essentially, identify the other companies who offer a service and specialty similar to yours, find out how they price their service, put yourself in the middle of that pack. As you develop your value proposition and book of successful projects you will be able to increase your fees.

The second method requires some thought, and a little math. You begin by figuring out what you want to make in the next year. If your goal is $80,000 you take this number and divide it by the number of hours you have available to work each year. To get this number you take the 52 weeks we have in a year. Subtract vacation time, holidays, family commitments, maybe even allow a few days that you might be ill during the year.

Let's say you are left with 49 weeks and you typically spend an average of 40 hours a week working. The calculation then is easy: 49 weeks times 40 hours equals 1960 hours available. New consultants will often go ahead and take this number and divide it by their goal salary. In this case it would be 80,000 / 1960 = $40.82 would be your hourly rate.

If you did this you are overlooking a significant issue:

you won't actually be working for your clients for 1960 hours a year. Why? Because you need to spend time on the marketing, administration and the general duties required to run and grow your consulting business.

For the purpose of creating a realistic pro forma for your business, here's what I suggest you do. Assume you'll be able to spend 50% of your time on actual client work. The 1960 hours is now reduced to 980 hours of billable work.

This means that your $80,000 as your goal salary divided by the 980 hours of billable work equals $81.63 an hour. This tells you is how much you need to work and at what per hour fee to be able to hit your goal of an $80,000 salary. If your goal is lower, your fee will be lower. If you want to spend less time but make the same amount of money, you'll need to raise your fee.

Let's not stop here because we should include another variable in our calculations. What about fixed your fixed and variable costs associated with running a business? If your annual overhead is $10,000 (rent, phone, internet, supplies, insurance, medical, etc) you'd take this number and divide it by the number of billable hours. In the above example it would be $10,000 / 960 = $10.42, So your previous rate of $88.88 would now be 81.63 + 10.42 = $92.05. Round that slightly up or down and your actual hourly rate is somewhere in the range of $90 to $100 an hour.

Having gone through this explanation, let me tell you it is extremely rare that you will ever bill on an hourly fee basis. It is important to keep this hourly number in the back of your mind, because you will be most frequently using one of these pricing models:

The Project Fee Model

You can move away from hourly work and into a project based fee structure. In this case you will need to determine how many hours you feel the project will take. I'd recommend adding an additional 50% or so to the expected hours you think it will take to complete the project. This allows for administration of the project and overflow. Put simply, things always take longer than you initially expect them to and you don't want to end up losing money on the project. This 'padding' gives you protection and is common practice among consultants. Adjust this additional percentage as needed. The fact is, even with project fees you still need to know what your hourly fee is so that you can estimate what it will take to complete the project.

The Daily Consulting Fee Model

Some consultants also prefer to bill by the day or half-day. There's nothing wrong with this approach and you'll still need to know what your hourly fee is so that you can calculate your daily fee.

For example, if your hourly fee is $200/hr and you'll be

spending 8 hours at your clients office you might charge $1600 for the day. But hold on a moment. There are a few other things for you to consider...

Travel Time: How long will it take you to reach your clients location? If it's only a few minutes, no big deal. But if you need to spend 1 hour each way to get there and back, that's 2 hours out of your day that you could otherwise be billing for. In that case, your 8 hour day has become a 10 hour day – and there is nothing wrong with you charging an extra $400 for the day to compensate you. Do you have to charge this? Of course not. That's completely up to you. But it's definitely worth considering.

Travel Expenses: If a company asks you to come and make a presentation at a location outside of your city or state they should pay for your travel costs. Want to travel business or first class? Now that all depends on your relationship with that client and how much of a name you've made for yourself. If you're well established in the industry and in high demand it's standard practice to ask for and expect business class travel. If you're just getting started building your name in the market you shouldn't expect business class travel, and I would recommend against asking for it.

The Value Calculation Fee Model

Now you have an idea of what kind of hourly fee you need to charge to earn the annual income you're after, and that means you know what you need to charge on a daily, weekly and monthly basis to achieve that. However, charging on an hourly or daily basis can only allow so much room for growth. If you want to be making $300,000 a year it's hard to ask a prospective client to pay you $1,000 an hour. Maybe you are worth that much, but most companies will be put off by a number like that and not retain you. Is there a way to generate a higher income for yourself without scaring away prospective clients?

Yes there is.

What about when a prospective client or even a current client says that your fees seem too high? Is there an effective way to deal with this? Again, yes there is.

The answer to both of these situations comes through a process of value calculation for your client, and then justifying your fees based not on hours, but on the value your client will receive from your services. When I use the term "value" I'm not referring to some sort of psychobabble about the intangibles I bring to the table. No, I'm talking measurable dollar value to the client for my services.

It took me a few years to learn how to do this properly, but my income has increased dramatically as a result. Your goal when negotiating fees is to get the right information early in the process, data from the customer about their business that will enable you to easily and dramatically demonstrate the true value of your work to them.

This all begins by asking the right questions. Let me give you an example that can be applied to every kind of consulting. For this example let's assume that I've been referred to an insurance business to help them grow sales. (Remember, this could be any kind of business and you could offer them any kind of service.) I meet with the President of the company, and in the course of our conversation I ask some very specific questions. These include:

1. How much is an average client worth to the company?
2. How many new clients are they attracting each month now?
3. How much are they currently spending to attract this new business?

With that information I can now craft a case of the value I will deliver. Let's say that the company currently estimates that each new client is worth $10,000 to them, that they currently bring in 10 new clients a month at a total marketing cost of $25,000. Now I know that they are bringing in roughly $100,000 in new business each month at a cost of $25,000, leaving a net of about $75,000 monthly of new business. Of course they have many other fees for their office, employees, and so on, but you get the idea.

The point here is all about demonstrating value and

justifying your fees. I tell the President my fees are $10,000 a month and that I typically start off with an agreement to work together for 4 months, but they can cancel at anytime if they are not satisfied. I don't stop just with stating my fee. Knowing what I now know, I say to the company that I expect we can lower their marketing and advertising costs by 50% (to $12,500 per month) through testing and tracking and they'll still see the same results in new business. I also expect that with improving their current ads and lead handling system, we can bring in an additional two clients each month (worth an additional $20,000 each month). I could keep going with this example and show them how I'd save them more money or make them more by using different strategies through the knowledge and experience I have.

The result is that I show the company how we can expect to make them an additional $32,500 each month. Of course, this won't happen right away, but maybe we agree that within 4 months of working together these will be the results. Now, if I'm making this company an extra 25 grand each month, or $300,000 a year (their gains minus my fee) don't you think they'd be more than happy to pay!

This is how you justify your fees through value calculation. You don't have to just increase sales; you can be reduce expenses, speed up a process, reduce lost time due to equipment failure or employee injury, or a myriad of other services that will result in improved financial performance for the company.

Always remember this face: business owners think in money. Whatever you use to show the value you will create, be sure to tie it back to what that means for them in dollars and cents.

The Pricing Model You Should Use Most Frequently

One of the biggest challenges you'll face as a consultant, especially in the early days, is making your income stable. Now, I don't mean that you get a check every 2 weeks as a typical employer would provide, but rather that you have a continuous flow of work. When you do hourly or project work, it often really is just that. You go to work, tackle whatever issue it is you're helping with, and once you're finished, it's over. You send the invoice, you get paid, and you don't hear from that client again until they need more work. Sounds good, right? Sure, it's standard practice.

The big problem with this is that you need to have an ever increasing pool of clients so that when one project is over you can go right to the next one. Some clients will only have a one-time project or they'll drop off for whatever reason. This means you will must be continuously adding to your client base.

Why a consulting retainer makes this better: When you set up a retainer agreement with your client, essentially you work with them for x amount of hours each month and bill them monthly. It really is as straightforward as that.

Here's what you need to do to make this all work:

1. You must have a plan for what will be accomplished each month. Or a clearly
defined set of deliverables that both you and the client have agreed on.

2. Each week or at minimum at each meeting with the client you should show them what has been achieved or completed prior to the meeting. That way they can see the progress and feel the momentum.

3. Always plan ahead. Again at each meeting, don't just review what you've completed. Review with your client what you plan to accomplish next. Depending on your client how formal these plans should be will vary. I've had some clients that require a status of the project every two weeks to one month with figures and data. Others just want to talk about it.

4. Deliver. This one's critical. I know it sounds basic, but the whole reason consulting retainers work is because you can make things happen and your client is willing to pay you on an ongoing basis to continue the work. The next time you're showing your client your fees or sending a proposal or bid for a project, be sure to build in an option for monthly retainer work.

The consulting retainer set up works better for both you and your client. You get the stability of having a few clients that provide you with steady work and income. And because you don't have to manage and chase down as many clients you can focus better on your clients' business, give them more of your time, and deliver better results.

Clients Love Pricing Plans

Clients love to have options. Don't you? One of the most effective pricing strategies you should consider is the pricing strategy of three. This is how it works:

You offer your clients 3 packages. You can call them bronze, silver and gold or anything else that makes sense for your business. The name isn't what's important, it's the concept and the psychology behind it that makes it work.

Your first offering is your bronze package. This is your least expensive plan and includes the fewest amount of hours you spend with your client or fewer deliverables.

The next plan up, we'll call the silver plan, is more expensive and goes beyond the basic services of your bronze plan. This one offers more value, more of your time or more deliverables.

The gold plan is the most expensive. This is your all-in, total support, complete high roller package. The cost isn't the only thing that increases with this plan, you'll deliver far more value to your client. Your time with them may increase, you may use better systems, or a wider advertising reach, or maybe you'll manage and implement more aspects of the strategy you've set. The key to this is that your prices increase as you deliver more and more value to your clients.

Remember, this shouldn't just be a bunch of frills and gimmicks, but actual services that your clients would find more valuable and helpful for their business. 70-80% of the time you'll find clients take the middle (silver) package. This is where the psychology kicks in. Most clients don't want 'the cheapest' and they find it hard to initially justify 'the most expensive' so they take the middle ground.

As a consultant this works out great for you. Neglecting to offer three plans often results in clients taking or not taking the only deal you offer them. Here you give them more choice and make the choice easier. I've seen offering 2 packages also work but I'd never offer more than 3. It gets too confusing and the last thing you want to do is complicate your clients purchase decision.

How Consultants Can Get Very Rich

There's only so much time in each day and only one of you. So how do you go from making a very good income to making an amazing income?

You partner with your client. Not in the legal sense of becoming an owner in the
business, but you agree to share in the revenues or savings generated as a result of your work. I've suggested this format a couple of times, and I'll tell you it's not the easiest thing to do well. But when it works, it's by far and away the best way to make an incredible income.

I first heard this strategy when I attended a three day workshop with the legendary Jay Abraham more than twenty years ago. He would only accept "partner clients" and limited himself to three new clients each year. He would evaluate their businesses and only work with a company that he felt would generate a minimum of $1 million net to him in the first year! I haven't don't that kind of number yet, but it's a goal!

Here's how it works. You agree with your client that you won't take any payments or fees for your work. In return, 20%-50% of the revenues or savings that you produce for your client's business are yours.

Why would your client turn over as much as 50% of their money to you? Because they don't have to put up anything in advance, and they only have to pay you when they make money. Sure, they may not make as much, but it's a sure thing and they will be happy knowing they have someone as part of their team that can produce results.

If you boost your client's business by $500,000 a year, $250K of that would be yours. Of course, you must have the confidence that you can produce results. If you can't you're just wasting your time. Sounds pretty good, right? Well, I did say that this isn't easy to work. The main reason is that you have to completely trust the client. If you don't have a solid relationship with them, the result is almost guaranteed to deliver you nothing but stress, frustration and little to no money.

What I recommend to consultants is that they work at least a project or two and successfully complete those with the client first. If all of that goes well then you're in a much better position to entertain the idea of partnering and sharing in the profits. This setup won't work for every kind of consulting business. But if it can work for yours, and it can work for many, it's definitely something you should explore as you begin working and completing successful projects.

Getting Clients

For the majority of consultants starting out, getting their first few of clients proves to be their most difficult task. It's understandable. Most don't know where to start. Where they can find the right clients, and then what should they say to them to win their business? To answer these important questions I'll want to share thoughts in three areas: getting prepared to meet with prospects, identifying your ideal prospects and marketing to this group of prospects.

Getting ready to meet with prospects

Just because you've decided to use your expertise in a field to become a consultant, doesn't mean you are ready to begin talking with prospects. Before you start setting appointments with prospective clients take the time necessary to answer these six questions:

1) Have you defined what makes you different than others in the market? Have you written this statement down and committed it to memory? This is your "value proposition" and you must be able to clearly state it if you want a prospect to consider retaining your services.

2) Have you generated results that will help you prove your skills? These might have come when working for a previous employer or helping a friend in their business. You want to have experience(s) you can point to that demonstrates you will be able to produce results for a client.

3) Have you clearly listed the services you can provide and how they will benefit the client? The key here is to focus on the benefit that your client will enjoy as a result of the service you are offering.

4) Do you have an understanding of the industry or concerns that face the company(s) you are targeting in your market? Do know the language of the industry? What is it that keeps your prospective client up at night,

and how can you help him/her?

5) Can you clearly explain how you price your services and the value you'll provide
that justifies their cost?

6) Are you ready to invest money in your business? Most consultants don't spend very much money on promoting their business. That's fine when you're already established and have a very strong presence in the market. But if you don't, you need to be prepared to spend some money on marketing and advertising. It doesn't have to be a lot. But the saying "it takes money to make money" does hold true.

Identifying Your Ideal Prospects

The secret to finding new clients is something I've talked about several times in this book: Focus. A big mistake is trying to market to every industry out there without any real criteria. This shotgun approach rarely provides the results you're after.

If you are fortunate enough to consult in a very specific niche where you can easily identify prospective clients then your marketing task is much easier. I'll share a quick example of this. I have a good friend who developed a specialty as a safety consultant in the energy industry. He conducts highly focused training for employees in oil and gas processing plants and nuclear energy plants. Since safety training in this industry is mandated by many governments, he has developed a successful, world-wide consulting business with repeat customers.

If you don't have the benefit of that level of specialization, there here is a formula to help you create a niche market for your services. Begin the process by identifying:

1. An industry you want to target. Obviously this should be a market that you have some familiarity with. You can't afford the time for a long learning process as you begin your business.

2. A location you want to target. Do you want to work primarily in your own city? Or, like my friend who does safety consulting, do you want to be available for clients in other cities or countries?

3. A size of company you want to target (either by employees or revenue). This is an important consideration because in most cases small companies will not understand the value that you offer, or be able to afford it.

Once you've determined your target market it's time to identify 100 prospects in that market. The late Chet Holmes called this strategy the "Dream 100" and used it to build several successful companies. How can you do this? Fortunately the internet has made this a much easier task. You can do a keyword search for companies in your category, then research each of the companies that you find. This may seem like a lot of work, but this activity will save you a great deal of time and money that you would waste chasing leads that are not a good fit for what you offer.

Another place to find this data is by subscribing to one of the data services like infoUSA (www.infousa.com) or SalesGenie (www.salesgenie.com). For a small monthly fee, you can access their entire database of more than 15 million businesses and identify your Dream 100. I have used both of these companies and like their service, but there are others you can consider as well. You can do a month-to-month contract so the expense is quite low for the simplicity they offer.

Why would you choose only 50 to 100 companies and forget about all the rest? Two reasons. First, most consultants can't handle working with more than 5-10 clients at one time, do you really need to go after 1000? Of course not. Second, it costs a lot more to keep marketing to hundreds or thousands of companies on a regular basis than a highly focused list of 100. (Go back and read chapter 9 if you doubt this.)

7 Marketing Methods That Consultants Use to Grow Their Business.

1. The 7 - 12 Step Campaign. I've read enough studies, and experienced it myself in business, that demonstrate it takes between seven and twelve "touches" of your marketing message to actually get through to your target prospect. Now that you have your Dream 100 in place, it is time to begin your campaign to them.

When I say "campaign" I mean that in the military sense. That is, a well thought out strategic series of marketing pieces designed to get you an appointment with the right person in the company. That's right, an appointment. Your first goal is just to get the opportunity to make a personal presentation to the decision maker who has the authority (and budget) to hire you.

Your campaign will be a combination of direct mail packages, emails, a copy of your newsletter or book, a CD with audio track of a presentation you've made, an invitation to a seminar where you are speaking, a report you've written. You get the idea. You are making the prospect aware of you, showing them that you are credible and a person worth meeting.

This is how you'll attack your Dream 100, but you are not limited to just trying to attract them as clients, especially as you're starting out your practice. Here are some other proven business growth strategies you can incorporate.

2. Networking. Attending events where other business people gather can be an effective method for introducing yourself and your services. Your local Chamber of Commerce will sponsor several of these each year, many are open to non-members for a small fee. You can also join networking groups as a way to meet people. When I started my business I joined a chapter of Business Networking International (BNI). My first seven clients came through BNI. If you're considering joining a group, make sure in advance that the group really does promote business leads. Some groups are service oriented and do not facilitate actually growing the businesses of their members. Also look for professional associations in the area of your expertise and join them.

3. Pay Per Click. Pay-per-click advertising has become especially effective as a method of getting found by the search engines. Competition for organic search results has become so difficult for a new company that paid advertising may be your only alternative. You can control the expense by paying careful attention to the keywords you select, and making sure you also identify negative keywords.

In the past year Facebook Pay Per Click has become a viable alternative to Google. The cost is almost always less on a per click or per impression basis, and Facebook offers an advertiser the ability to very precisely define their target market. They have recently introduced the "Power Editor" tool for advertisers, and continue to make updates to their paid advertising platform.

4. Print Advertising. General "image" advertising in newspaper or local magazines is often too expensive for most consultants, particularly when starting out. However, if you can identify publications that appeal directly to your Dream 100, and that they are likely to be reading, it can be worth the investment. Here are some tips if you do this:

- Create a black and white ad (it's less expensive)
- Run your initial ad in a smaller size, business card size for example
- Request that your ad be run at the top of the right hand page (or above the fold if it's online). This is scientifically proven to generate higher response. If you're a new advertiser they may not agree, but it's worth asking
- Try to work out a deal with the media rep at the publication so you can test running the ad for a couple weeks or months. During that time, try to change the headline and/or offer you make in the ad and see how that improves your response.

Advertising in trade (business) publications does work. It may take you some time to figure out the right formula of an effective ad in the right publication. But once you do, it can be a valuable marketing asset.

5. Direct Mail. I continue to read how direct mail is dead or dying and that you'd be a fool to spend money on it. Not true! If that was the case then why would one of the largest direct mailers in the US right now be Google? That's right. The 800# gorilla of online search spends hundreds of thousands of dollars on direct mail each year.

If you selected a list of Dream Clients and put together a multiple piece campaign to grab their attention, tell them your story and why they should care; and have a follow-up plan in place, direct mail will work for you.

The key with direct mail is getting the right message to the right person. You can get their attention by sharing with them some insights or knowledge you have into the industry, what dangers they face if they don't make some adjustments, or what they could be doing to improve their business. Speak their language and they'll listen.

Another reason that direct mail can work extremely well is due to what's happening online. More and more companies are shifting their marketing budgets to the online world. In many ways that's a great thing. It tends to be cheaper and easier to measure results. This increase in online marketing means there's a decrease in print (offline) marketing. With more and more marketing going online it means receiving a letter or package in the mail is less uncommon; it gets attention. That's right. Fewer people doing offline marketing also means that your efforts have less competition. And that's a great starting point to meeting and landing new clients.

6. Seminars. Seminars and workshops are a great way to get your message in front of a group of people at a very low cost. When you're starting out you can put on free seminars at a local library, chamber of commerce, or rotary club. Pretty much just about anywhere that will lend you a room.

It's always great if you can find n organization that already has an established
membership. They'll promote your seminar to their members and all you have to do is show up and give your talk. That is not to minimize the work involved in putting together a great seminar or workshop. This is one of the best ways to really demonstrate your expertise. If people like what you have to say, they'll invite you to speak at other locations, or will want to introduce you to someone they know. I've had these engagement lead to consulting jobs on more than one occasion.

When you've really got your presentation down pat and you've built up your confidence through a few trial runs, you can offer to put on a seminar or workshop for one of your dream clients. As with most marketing, your seminar shouldn't come across as a sales pitch. The best presentations don't focus on the person giving them nor the product or service they offer. The best presentations are educational, filled with facts, stories and new ideas.

7. Articles, Newsletters, Books. As a consultant you are going to be doing a great deal of writing, both for your own business and your clients. Writing articles for a local newspaper or website is a great way to get your name out there. Producing a newsletter focused on issues that are important to your target market will help establish you as a voice in the industry. Writing a book is a great way to establish your credibility.

A key to article writing and newsletter writing, whether online or in print, is to do it on an on-going basis. Writing something once or twice a year in any publication won't accomplish very much for you. Get your piece on a weekly or monthly basis and you'll start seeing some results. Just be sure to cover topics that would be of interest to your target market.

There is a big misconception that you have to have some sort of special credentials or permission to have your work published. Not true. In fact, most industry specific magazines and newsletters are always looking for new authors and articles. Share good value in each article and be sure to let your opinion shine through and you'll find many places that are interested in publishing your articles.

This is even more true if you write a book. Most authors make little or no money from publishing their books. But that's not the reason most people in business write a book. In business, a book is a credibility tool. Society has trained itself to believe that if someone is published or has self published a professional looking book they must be extremely smart. As a consultant if you have it in you to write a book that covers your area of expertise, it can be incredibly powerful.

Consider this scenario. A potential client contacts you and wants more information about your services. You either send them a copy of your book or point them towards it. That's about all the proof they'll need to accept you are an expert. Today there are quite a few services that make it very easy to self-publish your book.

Keeping Clients

A consultant's business is always a relationship business. Your level of success is directly connected to the level of service, satisfaction and happiness you provide your clients with. In short, they are the lifeblood of your business – and you'd be a fool to ever forget this.

Every month, when you client sits down to write the check and pay your invoice, they are asking themselves, "did I get \$____ in value from my consultant this month?" If they can't answer that question with a resounding YES for more an a month or two you will be out of a job. Worse than the short term loss of income, you have lost a source of testimonials and referrals.

Here are some strategies to incorporate into your practice management that will help you avoid lost clients.

1. Be responsive. How many times have you left a message for someone or sent them an email and they don't respond for days. In fact, YOU are the one that has

to follow up and get in touch with them. You never want your clients to have that experience with you.

In my personal experience, email is a great crutch that we use as a substitute for real communication. The fact is that most client issues stem from miscommunications, and often it is not being clear in an email that is the culprit. It could be something as simple as the fact that an email conversation may take several days to complete, and by then one of you has forgotten the original intent. Or it could be your client is upset and shoots off an email in haste.

I always pick up the telephone and call the client. First, I want to be sure I really understand their concern and talking on the phone helps me do that. It also gives both of an opportunity to address the issues, talk through possible solutions, and make decisions in real time. When in doubt, use the phone.

2. Do What You Promise. If you make a promise keep it. If you've told a client that you'll get them the report they've asked for by Thursday, send it by Thursday, if not earlier. Clients may not tell you this directly, but they judge everything you do.   Even in their subconscious their minds are forming opinions and feelings around the way you work. One of the easiest ways to keep your clients loyal is to meet and exceed their expectations

3. Spend Money on your Clients. A great way to keep

them on your side is by sending gifts and notes of appreciation. Too many consultants spend little to no money on their clients. This isn't about buying their business, it's about building and strengthening the relationship.

If you're getting paid, even just $1,000 a month from a client, that's $12,000 a year, would it be reasonable for you to spend $200-$400 a year showing them that you appreciate their business?

When I've enjoyed a real good meal out, I'll often go back to the restaurant and buy a few gift cards, attach a card to each and mail them to clients that I know would appreciate a nice evening out. In such cases I don't mention "thank you for your business" or say anything that could be interpreted as that sounds like you're trying to buy their happiness.

What I do is write a short note that says something like this, "John, we had a great meal at this restaurant and thought you might enjoy it too. By the way, I had the risotto. Regards, Gordon". That's it. Their first thought when they get that is, "Wow, that's nice of him." That's my goal. They think it's nice, and they appreciate knowing that I appreciate them. That's all part of building the relationship.

Little things like that throughout the year are a great way to differentiate yourself
from others in the market and to continue receiving

your clients' business. A couple times a year I may also send a larger basket. One with some tropical fruit and another with chocolates.

4. Regular Progress Reports. Progress reports are one of the most powerful ways to keep your clients happy, make sure the project is on track and keep the work coming. Most consultants are well intentioned and have a plan to provide regular progress reports– but they don't. A progress report is a simple (often one page) document that outlines three things:

1) What work has been completed and the results of that work.
2) What you are currently working on and its status.
3) What you'll be working on next (or suggest that you do) and the value it provides.

This three step process sounds very simple, and it is, but the effect it has is quite deep and powerful. Let's dig into each of the 3 parts of the progress report:

Part 1. When you tell your client what you've completed and show them the results, they feel good inside because it justifies them spending their money and shows they made a good decision hiring you. Of course if the results aren't good, you need to have a plan to explain why and how they'll be fixed.

Part 2. By showing them what you are currently working on and giving them a status update on that they can see that you are working hard and again it justifies continuing to pay you for your expertise.

Part 3. This is a big one. By showing what the next steps are, or giving recommendations for the next ones, you're setting your clients up to understand and see the value in your ongoing work. If you don't have any next steps planned out, figure some out that provide value to your client. It could be continued work on the same area of their business, or work on a new area. If you just focus on what you've agreed to do and don't work on lining up your next step of work your project will come to a swift end and you'll be leaving a great deal of money on the table.

Progress reports are extremely easy to put together. They can really be as simple as a few sections on a piece of paper with bullet points. Or a chart displaying results, or both. This is an often overlooked area of the consultant's role. But it's something you should definitely be doing on a regular basis. Since most of my clients are set up as a monthly retainer work, I provide them with progress reports on a monthly basis. However, since these reports only take a short time to put together, I can provide one quickly at anytime as needed.

What is My Opinion

As I've said several times, I have worked as a consultant for the past eleven years. Obviously I enjoy the profession and have found it to be profitable.

For the person with good experience in the area that they will consulting this is an excellent business model. It is not without risk, which is one of the reasons I have gone into the level of detail in this chapter that I did. With thoughtful planning and effective initial marketing of your practice, consulting can be a rewarding and profitable second career.

Gordon Van Wechel

Chapter 17   Putting it All Together

I belong to a Mastermind group. We are eight business owners and professionals who meet monthly to share what we are doing in our businesses, get feedback and advice from the other members, and hold each other accountable to do what we say we are going to. The facilitator of our group is a wise and experienced entrepreneur who has a lifetime of business experiences.

Each year he creates a "theme" for his group members, and we remind each other of it at our monthly sessions. This year's theme is: "if it is to be, it is up to me!" As I bring this book to a close, that is the message I want to convey to you. My purpose has been to share with you a process of analysis that can be applied to evaluating business opportunities. There comes a time when the analysis is complete and you have to launch. That is when this theme statement will be most important— when you realize deep in your gut that it's time to end the countdown and blast off.

In this closing chapter I want to leave you with one final list. It's not another business checklist of to do's. It's more a checklist of "to be's." I'm going to share some characteristics that are common to successful people in many fields, not just business. You should realize by now that I'm not one of those woo-woo psychobabble people; I'm pretty bottom line oriented. So I'm offering you this last list because I'm confident that it will help you select the right business, launch it successfully, and grow it to the level that satisfies your personal goals.

Here are six characteristics that I've identified as being common to successful people.

1. Successful people have a purpose for their lives

Living a meaningful life starts with a sense of purpose. Those who are both happy and successful in their endeavors have invested time considering their unique purpose in life and have designed their steps to walk towards that purpose. Successful people follow their purpose with great passion. They believe in themselves and their ideas. They don't worry about what others may say or think—they know what they care about and are deeply committed to it.

If you go back to the first chapter of this book, "Preparing To Go Into Business," I suggested you think about identifying what you really want in all areas of your life. We are more than just business people, and are called to accomplish more in our lives than to just build a business. When you understand your unique purpose you'll realize that your business is just a vehicle to help you accomplish that purpose. Congruence in your life, and success in your business, will follow that understanding.

2. Successful people get started

There are a multitude of reasons not to begin. The economy, family, payments, financing, and about any other excuse you can imagine can derail you before you even start. Successful people realize that there is never a better time than now, and that if they wait the "right time" will never come around.

If you're young, you have the best opportunity to acquire riches because you have time to compound your efforts. If you're not young, take inspiration from Ray Kroc who was 52 years old when he started McDonalds. Or Harlan Sanders who was 62 when he began driving around the country introducing people to his fried chicken recipe. A secret of successful people is that they are ready when the opportunity comes. They understand that good opportunities are infrequent, and they don't let them pass by.

The bottom line is this: the best time to start is today. Don't put it off.

3. Successful people make good financial decisions

That means they are realistic about the lifestyle that their business will support at this time. They reinvest in their businesses, scaling their growth in a manageable pattern. They are very careful about taking on debt. They test their marketing ideas before making a major financial commitment.

Part of this financial literacy is that they invest in themselves. They are readers of personal development and inspirational books. Dan Kennedy has a phrase he often shares: "poor people have big TV's, rich people have big libraries." It's true. Donald Trump, by most definitions a successful business person, is a voracious reader. He often has three books going at the same time, and all focused on developing his business and personal skills.

Have you read a book lately? What's on your nightstand right now? Or in your briefcase? What's the last book you read? If you have an iPad, or any of the tablets, do you download books to read when you're waiting for a meeting? Successful people do.

4. Successful people are open to new ideas, but they're also decisive

They are always open to and reviewing new information that might prove helpful, but do not quickly change their course of action once begun. You may be surprised to learn that successful people are risk takers, but only after careful calculation of the odds for success. The image of the business person as a rash, Wild West gunslinger is just not true—at least not for the successful ones.

The Chinese have a proverb that says a person should be quick to make a decision and slow to change it. That describes successful people. They don't sit on the fence for long, but decide and move forward. Once moving, they are not distracted by the latest trend or "bright shiny object" that appears.

5. Successful people identify systems and repeat them over and over

Average people trade hours for dollars. If you have a particular skill, say an orthopedic surgeon, you might become well off by doing that. However, you will not become rich. Becoming rich requires leverage and a well oiled system.

What is the primary characteristic of a franchise opportunity? Their systems. If you are an entrepreneur who wants to create wealth you'll need to identify, test, and then duplicate a system for your business.

There is another component: building a team. Sam Walton was a master at sharing his vision with others who then became integral parts of the "WalMart Team." Even today, twenty years after his death, a significant reason for the companies dominance of the retail world is their emphasis on team building and empowering key people that was created by Mr. Walton in the early days.

6. Successful people are persistent, consistent, and patient. They work hard

Ray Kroc, Harlan Sanders, and Sam Walton didn't become rich overnight. Neither will you. Success takes time to build. Successful and happy people understand the process, the journey, and relish it. They know that there is a flow to life and seldom waste energy beating against that natural current.

They also recognize the need for hard work to accomplish their goals. I heard a speaker a few years ago who shared the story of how his business had finally taken off after more than 15 years. Someone came up to him after a speech he had given and commented that he was some sort of "overnight success." The speaker's response was, "that was the longest night in history."

Successful people don't have the words "give up" in their vocabulary. They realize that success really is 98% showing up every day and 2% talent.

Tom Watson, the visionary who built IBM into the greatest company of his day said, "would you like me to give you a formula for success? It's quite simple, really.

Double your rate of failure. You are thinking of failure as the enemy of success, but it isn't at all. You can be discouraged by failure or you can learn from it. So go ahead and make mistakes. Make all you can. Because remember that's where you will find success."

What Do I Think?

At this point you have an approach for your business: ready—aim—fire. Now it's time to take off the bib and put on the apron. Bib's are for people who want to be fed and for those not yet ready or willing to feed themselves. Aprons are for those who don't mind getting their hands dirty. Aprons are for those willing to take responsibility. Aprons are for those who, having made a decision to do something, manage their decisions each and every day.

It's time to put on your apron!

Gordon Van Wechel

ABOUT THE AUTHOR

Gordon Van Wechel is an entrepreneur who has built three national companies, each in a different industry. He has written three books, numerous articles and training manuals. He is a frequent speaker to business groups, and teaches a marketing class to new business owners for the Service Corps of Retired Executives (SCORE) division of the Small Business Administration.

In addition to his own enterprises, Mr. Van Wechel has travelled extensively in Asia and Africa on behalf of several Non-Government Organizations. His work focused on a micro-enterprise program that resulted in the creation of over 50 successful businesses, three schools, and numerous community development projects.

He is currently the President of The Alchemy Consulting Group, a marketing strategy and business growth firm based in Albuquerque, NM.

Gordon Van Wechel

The 11 Most Asked Questions About Working With The Alchemy Consulting Group

(and 11 great reasons why you'll jump at the chance to get your business rocketing forward.)

1. So Who is The Alchemy Consulting Group?

Alchemy is a strategic marketing and business growth consulting firm started in 2010 by Jennine Michael and Gordon Van Wechel. It is an outgrowth of a consulting practice that Gordon first began in 2003. Between them, Jennine and Gordon have over 60 years of hands on experience as entrepreneurs, building and selling several businesses of their own. The same is true of all of our associate consultants, who are experienced business owners. That means we know what it's like to work 80 hours a week and "wear all the hats" in the business.

Unlike most ad agencies or more traditional consulting firms, Alchemy has created a menu of services, we call them "modules." These have been designed to provide our clients with specific solutions to their business growth challenges regardless of how long you might have been in business. Whether you are the owner of a new business just starting out, or have an established company looking to expand, we can offer tools and strategies to help you take the next step. The benefit to you is that we don't expect you to fit into our "marketing mold." We will be able to help you evaluate exactly what you need, and can afford, at this time in your business.

2. Why Do I Even Need a Consultant?

Every great sports star, business person, and superstar is surrounded by coaches and advisors. As the world of business moves faster and gets more competitive, it can be difficult to keep up with the changes in your industry as well as the innovations in marketing and management. Having a business growth consultant is no longer a luxury; it's become a necessity.

If you're honest, you know that it is almost impossible to get an objective answer from yourself. That is not to say that you cannot survive in business without a consultant, but it's almost impossible to thrive.

A consultant can see the forest for the trees. A consultant will make you focus on the game, making you run more laps than you feel like. A consultant will tell it like it really is. A consultant will give you small pointers. A consultant will listen, and understand your pain. A consultant will help you remember the dreams you had when going into business...and help you get back on track to achieving them.

3. OK, so What is the First Step?

We'll ask you to complete our Marketing Audit. This is a series of questions, most of them are simple Yes/No answers, but there are several questions that will require a more detailed response. The purpose of the audit is to help you pinpoint areas of strength in your marketing now, and help identify those aspects of your plan that could use further work. A common experience of people participating in this exercise is a lot of ideas and excitement about what can be done to bring in more customers and profits. It will also prompt some questions about specific marketing tactics and how to implement them.

Once you have returned your audit, we'll schedule a time to meet together. This typically is a 60 to 90 minute conversation where we help you dig deeper into the level your company is performing at today, and where you'd like it to be in twelve months. It is also an opportunity for you to get to know us a little more, and see if working together makes sense. At the end of this meeting, at your request, we will prepare a proposal detailing our recommendations specific to your company, and the investment you will be making. You can then decide when you'd like to begin.

There is no charge for this initial meeting.

4. What Will You Do, and How Long Will it Take?

Just as every person is different, we believe each business is different. The plan that we suggest for your business will be based on the evaluation we make after reviewing your Marketing Audit and the conversation we have in the initial meeting. Which is to say that I cannot give you a specific idea of what we will do in your business, because we haven't designed your plan yet.

I can tell you that while about 80% of our strategic marketing focus today is online, we still incorporate traditional offline tools like direct mail and telephone marketing. We do that because they work. The particular mix of strategies for your company will depend on your goals, current situation, budget, competitive landscape, and personnel available to handle an influx of new customers.

Here's something else. Part of the Marketing Audit considers your current capacity. That is, how much more business can you handle well? It is no value to your business suddenly bring in 100 new clients when you only have the staff to properly serve 15 of them. We call this evaluating the "inside reality" of your company and is included in our modules.

As far as how long a typical program might take, we like to make commitments in 12 month increments. We don't try to lock someone in a contract saying that, but the plan we design for you will be based on a year of implementation.

If you've been in business for more than a few months you've already seen, and maybe even purchased, one or more so called "quick fixes." Most consultants want you to believe that they can solve your business growth problems in a few days. Our philosophy at Alchemy is that establishing a foundation for long term success in your business means not just scraping the surface with a few "Google secrets." We prefer to design a multi-channel marketing strategy that offers you controlled growth. That means implementing one or two modules initially, then, as they pay for themselves, adding more marketing. Over the course of a year, working together, we help you fully capitalize on current markets for your product/service, and extend the reach of your company into new areas.

5. How Do You Know This Will Work in My Industry?

Really simple. Our team of consultants are experts in sales, marketing, business development, management strategies, hiring key people, and evaluation of markets; just to name a few of their competencies. With more than 250 business building tactics in our arsenal you will quickly see how effective and powerful our modules are.

Add to this the fact that we have consulted with more than 300 companies in over 50 business categories and you can see that very likely that we have worked in a business that is the same or very similar to yours.

6. How Much Time and Money will This Cost Me?

The first couple of months your involvement in the processes will require more time. That might be review of copy or collateral materials, training your team in a new sales system, or regularly scheduled update meetings you'll have with one of our team members. The actual implementation of tactics, what we call the "back office fulfillment" duties, are all done by one of our groups of specialists. If part of your program calls for a revision of your website, the actual work will be done by our web builders. If you are doing a Real Time Bidding program, then another of our teams will handle the day to day details of that marketing channel for you.

As to the financial investment...well, nothing! That is if you look at it from the same perspective as we do. That's the difference between a cost and an investment. Everything we propose for your company is a true investment in your future. Not only will you create great results in your business, but you'll learn more than just marketing strategies. Working with our consultants will give you an education from experienced entrepreneurs you could never get in school, and this is knowledge that you can repeat over and over.

So you don't think I'm dodging the question, let me give you a range. We have clients who invest as little as $500 monthly and others who spend $10,000 a month. It will depend on your company, budget, short and long term growth goals, and how aggressively you want to pursue them.

7. Are There Any Guarantees?

Will all of your business goals be met by working with us? Maybe, or maybe not. We will never promise any specific result, nor can we guarantee that any of your goals will become a reality. The bottom line is we are your consultants, but it is still your business and it's up to you and your team to take the sales opportunities we bring you and convert those prospects to customers and eventually to raving fans of your business.

Only *you* can be fully accountable for your success. We guarantee to give you the best service we can, the benefit of all our experience and proven business growth strategies, and to encourage and even cajole you to reach for your goals. But at the end of the day it is your business.

Here is the guarantee that we do offer. When we work with you to design a strategic plan we'll define some clear goals that should be achieved within the first four months of working together. If they have not been achieved in that time period then we will continue to work with you at no charge until those goals have been met.

8. You're Based in Another City, How Does That Work?

You may have read Thomas Friedman's book from a few years ago called "The World Is Flat." His point was that with the communication tools available today business has truly become international. Even the shoe store down the street can have an ecommerce website or a store on eBay and sell to the whole world. Our business is living proof of that new reality: 80% of our clients live in another state. We regularly supply them with reports and updates via email, and schedule progress review conversations using phone or Skype.

Occasionally a client will want us to be at their location for a specific purpose, but generally that is an expense that you don't need to incur.

9. Do You Just Help With My Marketing?

While our primary focus is on marketing and business growth strategies, we'll help you in other areas too. For example, part of our Reputation Marketing module includes a training program helping your staff become more adept at customer service. I mentioned earlier the concept of the "inside reality" of your company, we'll help you identify operations within your business that can be improved.

We strongly believe in systems, the more you can implement systems in your business the better you can run your business instead of having it run you!

10. When is The Best Time to Get Started?

Yesterday. Really.

OK, right now, today; before you take another marketing step, waste another dollar, lose another sale, work another 70 hour week.

Far too many business people wait and see. They confuse activity with accomplishment and think that working harder will make it all better. Remember, what you know got you to where you are. To get to where you want to go you've got to make some changes and most likely learn something new.

There is no time like the present to get started on your dreams and goals.

11. How Do I Start?

Call us toll free at 877-978-2110 and ask for a Marketing Audit. You'll be connected with one of our consultants who will help you get started. We'll set up a time for an interview so we can learn about your business. Then we'll work with you to create a plan that helps you achieve your goals on a timeline that is affordable and makes sense for your business.

This may seem like a big job at the beginning, but with an Alchemy Consultant you'll have someone guiding you each step of the way.

Could You Profit From A Free, One Hour Flash Consultation Focused On Your Business?

I want to thank you for buying this book, and if you've found this page it means you probably even read most of it. The Ten Vital Questions are designed to help you identify the best business for you to go into. Once you've done that, how do you grow that business? That's what we do at The Alchemy Consulting Group, help our clients grow their companies to meet their goals.

Would you like to talk about your business? Whether you are still in the planning stages, or have been operating for years, I'd like to offer you a free, one hour "flash consulting" session.

What that means is a very quick, 10,000 foot view of your company and current marketing efforts. We'll ask a lot of questions, and answer yours. We might point you in a new direction, suggest a strategy that you hadn't considered, or help you look at what you're now doing in a new light.

This is a conversation about marketing and your business…it is not a thinly disguised pitch for you to hire us. Never once have I had anyone say it wasn't worth their time!

To take advantage of this offer you have to do a couple of things:

1. go to www.TheAlchemyConsultingGroup.com/flashconsult

2. answer the questions and give us your contact info

3. we'll call and schedule an hour that works for both of us to meet by telephone

4. come to our meeting with an open mind, a pen and pad ready to take notes, and be in a quiet place where you will not be interrupted.

I look forward to talking with you.

Gordon

www.ingramcontent.com/pod-product-compliance
Lightning Source LLC
Chambersburg PA
CBHW051444170526
45166CB00001B/102